The Harlem Group of Negro Writers

Recent Titles in
Contributions in Afro-American and African Studies

Willis Richardson, Forgotten Pioneer of African-American Drama
Christine Rauchfuss Gray

Critical Essays on Alice Walker
Ikenna Dieke, editor

Education and Independence: Education in South Africa, 1658–1988
Simphiwe A. Hlatshwayo

African American Autobiography and the Quest for Freedom
Roland L. Williams, Jr.

The White Image in the Black Mind: A Study of African American Literature
Jane Davis

Black Leadership for Social Change
Jacob U. Gordon

Mythatypes: Signatures and Signs of African/Diaspora and Black Goddesses
Alexis Brooks De Vita

African Visions: Literary Images, Political Change, and Social Struggle in Contemporary Africa
Cheryl B. Mwaria, Silvia Federici, and Joseph McLaren, editors

Voices of the Fugitives: Runaway Slave Stories and Their Fictions of Self-Creation
Sterling Lecater Bland, Jr.

Meditations on African Literature
Dubem Okafor

Achebe the Orator: The Art of Persuasion in Chinua Achebe's Novels
Chinwe Christiana Okechukwu

Rethinking the Slave Narrative: Slave Marriage and the Narratives of Henry Bibb and William and Ellen Craft
Charles J. Heglar

The Harlem Group of Negro Writers

Melvin B. Tolson

Edited by Edward J. Mullen

Contributions in Afro-American and African Studies, Number 203

GREENWOOD PRESS
Westport, Connecticut • London

Library of Congress Cataloging-in-Publication Data

Tolson, Melvin Beaunorus.
The Harlem group of Negro writers / by Melvin B. Tolson ; edited by Edward J. Mullen.
p. cm.—(Contributions in Afro-American and African studies, ISSN 0069–9624 ; no. 203)
Includes bibliographical references and index.
ISBN 0–313–31187–0 (alk. paper)
1. American literature—Afro-American authors—History and criticism. 2. Afro-Americans—New York (State)—New York—Intellectual life—20th century. 3. American literature—New York (State)—New York—History and criticism. 4. American literature—20th century—History and criticism. 5. Harlem (New York, N.Y.)—Intellectual life—20th century. 6. Harlem Renaissance. I. Mullen, Edward J., 1942– II. Title. III. Series.
PS153.N5T64 2001
810.9'89607307471—dc21 00–049073

British Library Cataloguing in Publication Data is available.

Library of Congress Catalog Card Number: 00–049073

ISBN: 0–313–31187–0
ISSN: 0069–9624

First published in 2001

Greenwood Press, 88 Post Road West, Westport, CT 06881
An imprint of Greenwood Publishing Group, Inc.
www.greenwood.com

Printed in the United States of America

The paper used in this book complies with the Permanent Paper Standard issued by the National Information Standards Organization (Z39.48–1984).

P

In order to keep this title in print and available to the academic community, this edition was produced using digital reprint technology in a relatively short print run. This would not have been attainable using traditional methods. Although the cover has been changed from its original appearance, the text remains the same and all materials and methods used still conform to the highest book-making standards.

Copyright Acknowledgments

The author and publisher gratefully acknowledge permission for use of the following material:

Melvin B. Tolson's thesis and excerpts from his papers used with permission of Melvin B. Tolson, Jr.

"I Have a Rendezvous with Life,""Yet Do I Marvel," and "To John Keats, Poet at Springtime" from *Caroling Dusk* by Countee Cullen, New York, Harper, 1927. Copyrights held by Amistad Research Center. Administered by Thompson and Thompson, New York, N.Y.

"Aesthete in Harlem," "Dark Youth of the USA," "Po'boy Blues," and "Cross" from *Collected Poems* by Langston Hughes. Copyright © 1994 by the Estate of Langston Hughes. Reprinted by permission of Harold Ober Associates Incorporated and Alfred A. Knopf, a Division of Random House, Inc.

Excerpts from *Melvin B. Tolson, 1898–1966: Plain Talk and Poetic Prophecy* by Robert M. Farnsworth reprinted by permission of the University of Missouri Press. Copyright 1984 by the Curators of the University of Missouri.

Excerpts from letters to the editor by Irwin S. Johnson, John Grimball Wilkins, and Doris Stead published in "The Sound and the Fury," *Esquire*, Vol. 1 (May 1934), p. 15 and Vol. 1 (June 1934), p. 166 used by permission of *Esquire*.

for Helen, Brian, Kathy, and Julie

Contents

Preface

The present edition of Melvin B. Tolson's study, "The Harlem Group of Negro Writers," reprints in its entirety the full text of Tolson's master's thesis, which he submitted to the Department of English and Comparative Literature at Columbia University in June 1940. With the exception of Chapter IV, which I reprinted in my *Critical Essays on Langston Hughes* (1986), the full text has never been reprinted and remains largely inaccessible. The present edition is based on a xerographic copy of the original typescript that Tolson submitted to Columbia University.

In addition to a negative of the original, which is held in the Preservation Division of the Columbia University Library, there is also a copy of Tolson's thesis in the Papers of Melvin Tolson, which are housed in the Manuscript Division of the Library of Congress. Tolson's papers, which consist of approximately 4,000 items, span the years 1932 to 1975 with the majority of the material dated 1940 to 1966. The collection consists primarily of literary manuscripts and drafts along with correspondence and notes that relate to literary matters. The Tolson papers also contain other items, particularly a correspondence series, which helps to illuminate the thesis. This consists of letters to friends and literary figures and also a series of book reviews and other kinds of ephemera that occasionally contain reference to his days in Harlem. The collection is carefully described in *Melvin Beaunorus Tolson: A Register of His Papers in the Library of Congress*, which is housed in the Manuscript Division of the Library of Congress. The compilers took note of the relationship of the collection to the study of African-American literature in general:

> The collection provides source material on Tolson's works and on the literary, artistic, and social legacy of the Harlem Renaissance. Since Tolson

> was born in 1898 and came of age as a poet along with the rise of black consciousness throughout the world, his papers represent a synthesis of African-American experience of self definition and ethnic cultural expression in early to mid-twentieth century America. Tolson's papers reflect the ideas embodied in negritude and often focus on race relations, African-American art and artists, and related social issues. (4)

A more general description of the papers is found in "Frontiers: Recent Acquisitions of the Manuscript Division," published in *The Quarterly Journal of the Library of Congress,* 33.4 (1976): 356–66.

The thesis consists of 139 pages of typescript. It opens with a one-page preface, in which Tolson presented the parameters of his study:

> There are three aims in this thesis: first, to give the social background of the Harlem Renaissance and the various forces that scholars say operated in the black metropolis to bring about the artistic and literary development of "The New Negro"; second, to emphasize the lives and works of the leading contemporary Negro essayists, short story writers, novelists and poets, in the light of modern criticism; and third, to interpret the attitudes and stylistic methods discovered in the Harlem Renaissance. (4)

The introductory commentary is followed by fourteen titled chapters. The first two, "A Perspective of Harlem" (5–10) and "The Negro or Harlem Renaissance" (11–17), serve as a backdrop to the study proper that analyzes the works of eleven African-American writers (Countee Cullen, Langston Hughes, Claude McKay, Walter White, Eric Walrond, Rudolph Fisher, Jessie Fauset, George Schuyler, W.E.B. Du Bois, James Weldon Johnson, and Wallace Thurman). The study ends with a twenty-two–page, three-part bibliography, itself a remarkable tool since it offers contemporary readers a list of citations emblematic of the critical practices of the time.

Tolson's "The Harlem Group of Negro Writers" is a document of considerable importance for the study of the Harlem Renaissance. Since it is the first history of one of the most significant moments in African-American literature of the twentieth century, it is hoped that an edition of Tolson's study will fill an important void in the source materials available to scholars and students of African-American and diasporic studies. The Harlem Renaissance was a period of extraordinary creative output by

African Americans, which is without parallel in American letters. It has also become the object of serious study and constant re-evaluation in recent years by the academic community. An edition of Tolson's unique evaluation of the movement forms part of a larger project of literary recovery typified by studies such as Cary D. Wintz's seven-volume *The Harlem Renaissance, 1920–1940,* the goal of which is to reprint articles and other materials that offer students and scholars the sources with which to assess and better understand the Harlem Renaissance. What makes Tolson's work so unique is that it was written by a writer who was both a participant in the movement and a committed literary critic. Tolson's evaluation of the renaissance was not only the result of lived experience but was also an academic thesis and thus a product of institutional criticism. Because of Tolson's personal connections with the writers he studied, the text is buttressed with letters and interviews with major African-American writers such as Eric Walrond, Wallace Thurman, and Rudolph Fisher. The inclusion of this material in Tolson's thesis makes it a remarkable document in African-American literary historiography.

Melvin Tolson (1898–1966) is an important but undervalued figure within the context of American literature whose fame rests largely on four books of poetry: *Rendezvous with America* (1944), *Libretto for the Republic of Liberia* (1953), *A Gallery of Harlem Portraits* (1979), and *Harlem Gallery: Book 1, The Curator* (1965). He also published a newspaper column, "Caviar and Cabbage," which appeared in the *Washington Tribune* from October 9, 1937, to June 24, 1944. At the time of his death in 1966, he was virtually unknown among scholars of American literature and a great deal of what he had written had either gone out of print or was largely unavailable to the reading public. The initial phase of his recovery began when in 1972 Roy P. Basler, then chief of the Manuscript Division of the Library of Congress, sent an essay, "The Heart of Blackness—M. B. Tolson's Poetry" to the journal *New Letters,* a quarterly published by the University of Missouri-Kansas City. David Ray, the editor, asked Robert Farnsworth, a professor of American literature, to read the manuscript. Farnsworth, fascinated with the work of Tolson, then agreed with Tolson's wife Ruth to begin to seek appropriate publication outlets for many unpublished manuscripts, which were now housed in the Library of Congress. In 1979, Farnsworth published Tolson's *A Gallery of Harlem Portraits,* a collection of poems that Tolson completed in 1935 but for which he was never successful in finding a publisher. In 1982, Farnsworth edited selected columns Tolson had written for the *Washington Tribune* under the title *Caviar and Cabbage: Selected Columns.* The project to recover Tolson continues well into the present. In 1999, the University Press of Virginia published *"Harlem Gallery" and Other Poems of Melvin B. Tolson.* The book, edited by Raymond Nelson with an introduction by Rita Dove, reprints in their entirety *Rendezvous with America* (1944), *Libretto for the Republic of Liberia* (1953), *Harlem Gallery* (1965), and five fugitive poems: "African China," "A Long Head to a Round Head," "The Man from Halicarnassus," "E. & O. E.," and "Abraham Lincoln of Rock Spring Farm."

Because I consider "The Harlem Group of Negro Writers," somewhat akin to Langston Hughes's *The Big Sea* (1940), to be the most readable study of the renaissance years, every effort has been made to let Tolson's voice speak for itself. To that end, the text has been reprinted in a style consistent with the original with the footnotes set at the bottom of the page. I have corrected obvious misspellings and basic errors in some citations by supplying correct page and volume numbers. Occasionally Tolson incorrectly transcribed the titles in some of his citations. In such cases, I have inserted the correct title in brackets. I regret that I was unable to locate the following sources as Tolson cited them: *American's News, Independent Book Review, Editorial,* and *Minnesota Student.* The editorial glosses that appear in brackets after Tolson's original notes are intended to clarify and expand upon issues that may be unclear to the contemporary reader. The introductory essay is designed to offer both a historical and interpretive frame from which to read Tolson's study. It is divided into four parts: a brief bio-bibliographic overview, a discussion of the major studies written about Tolson, a history of the writing of the thesis, and finally general observations on the relation of Tolson's study to other studies of the renaissance and his use of sources. Since from their inception African-American literary studies have been marked by a series of debates, largely linked to the question of race and cultural identity, Tolson's positions on these issues will be examined in considerable detail.

This study ends with a two-part bibliography: the first supplies bibliographic information about Tolson scholarship; the second is a selected bibliography of the Harlem Renaissance. The latter does not attempt to be complete since more comprehensive bibliographies are available elsewhere, namely Margaret Perry's *The Harlem Renaissance: An Annotated Bibliog-*

raphy and Commentary (1982) and Robert A. Russ's "The Harlem Renaissance: A Selected Bibliography," which appears in *Harlem Renaissance Re-Examined: A Revised and Expanded Edition* edited by Victor A. Kramer and Robert A. Russ (1997). There are electronic online sources as well, such as Paul P. Reuben's "Chapter 9: Harlem Renaissance—Selected Bibliography," which is found in *PAL: Perspectives in American Literature: A Research and Reference Guide* (URL: *http://www.csustan.edu/english/reuben/pal/chap9/biblio.html*) as well as online citations from the online *MLA International Bibliography.* The selective bibliography on the Harlem Renaissance also contains the complete bibliographic information to all citations in the glosses to Tolson's thesis.

Acknowledgments

I wish to express my appreciation to the Research Board of the University of Missouri for funding a Summer Research Fellowship during which I was able to travel to the Library of Congress to consult the Tolson papers. In particular I would like to acknowledge with gratitude the advice, encouragement, and help given to me by Marvin Lewis, Flore Zéphir, and Miriam DeCosta-Willis. I owe special thanks to Benjamin Honeycutt who very carefully read the Introduction to this book. I appreciate the assistance of Mr. Andrew Jewell, who helped with the final preparation of the manuscript and is largely responsible for the bibliography. I am grateful to the staff at Ellis Library for their help in securing materials from other libraries. I appreciated the assistance of Junko Stuveras of the Columbia University Libraries and Bradley E. Gerand, senior archivist at Library of Congress, for the help with questions concerning sources. Thanks is due to Arnold Rampersad for identifying individuals to contact concerning permissions; to Cynthia Mercado, Kara Seidel, and Mary Harris who typed portions of the manuscript, and to Andrew Berry of Letra Libre who was responsible for the typography and design of this book.

This project would not have been possible without the earlier work of other Tolson scholars. A special debt is due to Robert Farnsworth, without whose patience and hard work much of the writing of Melvin B. Tolson might still remain undiscovered.

Grateful acknowledgment is given to Melvin B. Tolson, Jr., for permission to edit "The Harlem Group of Negro Writers."

Introduction

Melvin B. Tolson: An Overview

Although the primary focus of this study is the period Tolson spent in Harlem, I have elected to provide a thumbnail sketch of his life and works in order to provide the reader with an overview, albeit brief, of his contribution to American letters. Melvin Beaunorus Tolson was born in 1898 in New Franklin, Missouri, the son to Alonzo and Elra Tolson. His father was a self-educated minister who worked for the Methodist Episcopal Church. Robert Farnsworth, Tolson's biographer, described Alonzo in the following way:

> The Methodist tradition with which Alonzo vigorously identified himself supported the values of learning as well as those of morality. Alonzo lived according to that tradition and passed those values on to his son. Although he only completed the eighth grade, he took a number of correspondence courses and taught himself Latin, Hebrew, and Greek. His independent educational efforts apparently made him skeptical of the value of a formal college education, and Melvin always credited his mother with encouraging him to go to Fisk and Lincoln Universities. (*Plain Talk* 7)

More is known about Tolson's mother whom he described in an early essay entitled "The Odyssey of a Manuscript." She imbued in him a strong sense of racial pride, which is evident from the essay's first lines: "But my little walnut-hued mother taught me not to cry when hurt by the slings and darts of the white man's civilization. She was the descendant of very colored fugitives who hid themselves in the islands in the Mark Twain country in the glooms of the Ozarks, from which they raided the slave plantations along the Missouri and the Mississippi. They were a taciturn, hot-blooded clan that produced gun-toting preachers and praying bad men. . . . The little walnut-hued woman was fiercely proud of being an American Negro, although in her veins flowed Irish, French, Indian, and African blood" ("The Odyssey" 4).

Tolson was raised primarily in Missouri, although the family did live briefly in Oskalloosa and Mason City, Iowa. He attended Lincoln High School in Kansas City, Missouri, where he began his career as a writer with two short poems ("The Past, Present, and Future" and "Retrospection") and two short pieces of fiction ("Wonders in the Sierra" and "The Cabin's Victim"), which were published in the high school yearbook *The Lincolnian,* in 1917 and 1918, respectively (*Plain Talk* 20). After graduating from high school, he enrolled at Fisk University in Nashville, Tennessee. After his freshman year, he transferred to Lincoln University, where he majored in journalism and theology. He married Ruth Southall in 1922 and graduated in June 1923, the same month that saw the birth of his first son, Melvin, Jr. Tolson's studies at Fisk and Lincoln were to have a profound, shaping effect on his life as a writer and teacher. Both schools, founded after the Civil War, were among the most prestigious African-American universities in the United States. Lincoln was the oldest (it was founded in 1859) and had been a magnet for the formation of the African-American intelligentsia in the early 1920s. Among its alumni are such distinguished figures as Dr. Horace Mann, Thurgood Marshall, Nnamdi Azikiwe, Kwame Nkrumah, and Langston Hughes, who is widely regarded as the most important writer of the Harlem Renaissance and a friend of Tolson. Soon after graduation, Tolson secured a job at Wiley College in Marshall, Texas, and began a virtually uninterrupted career as a college professor for the next forty-one years of his life. With the exception of the academic year 1931–32, when he was studying at Columbia University for his master's degree, Tolson remained at Wiley until the late forties. In 1924, he organized the Forensic Society and began a career as a debating coach, which would hone his skills as a public speaker, expand his contacts both within and without the African-American community, and form lasting and important bonds with students, such as Hobart Jarrett, who would later become major figures in African-American literary scholarship in their own right. Tolson remained at Wiley from 1923 until 1947 when he accepted a position at Langston University in Langston, Oklahoma.

By the late 1930s, Tolson had written a good deal of verse, two plays, many newspaper columns, and two novels in draft form. Tolson's first book, *A Gallery of Harlem Portraits,* a series of poems described by Farnsworth as "relatively crude, but often strong and immediate in its impact" (*A Gallery* 257) was most probably begun in 1932 but not completed until 1935. Tolson described the genesis of the collection and provided a glimpse into the frustrations of the author-publisher relationship in his classic "The Odyssey of a Manuscript." The model for the project was most probably Edgar Lee Masters' *Spoon River Anthology.* Tolson wrote: "It is a poem similar to Masters' *Spoon River Anthology,* with Harlem as a magnet drawing characters of diversified types from all corners of the world. It gives, I think, Negro America, [*sic*] its comedy and tragedy, in prismatic epitome" (qtd. in Russell 10). The two hundred portraits finally achieved print in 1979 in an edition prepared by Robert Farnsworth.

Tolson's first full-length book, *Rendezvous with America,* would not appear until 1944. Published in the twilight years of the Second World War by Dodd, Mead and Company, it was to mark his entrance, albeit tardily, into the arena of mainstream American letters. *Rendezvous with America* is not an organic book of poetry but rather a collection of poems that he brought together at the request of Mary Lee Chamberlain, an editor at *Atlantic Monthly*—a magazine that had published Tolson's "Dark Symphony." The latter had been awarded the National Poetry Contest Prize sponsored by the American Negro Exhibition in Chicago in 1940. The slim volume, divided into eight sections, contains four long poems: "Rendezvous with America," "Dark Symphony," "The Idols of the Tribe," and "Tapestries of Time." The remainder of the book consists of groupings of less thematically related poems. The book's publication is not surprising given the nation-building efforts of the late 1940s. In a tone somewhat reminiscent of W.E.B. Du Bois's "Close Ranks," the title poem "Rendezvous with America" foregrounds a sense of optimism. While it is apparent that the predominant time frame is the present, that is, the final years of World War II, the text treats American history from its beginnings at Plymouth Rock to the attack on Pearl Harbor. "Dark Symphony," as the title suggests, was a text more firmly grounded in the African-American culture. The poem, chronicling as it does the achievements of African Americans and locating them within the broader tradition of democratic American society, is not only consistent with the ideological assumptions of the time, but had sufficient ethnic character to make it an extremely appealing text to the broader American readership. Robert Farnsworth's comments are germane: "The democratic promise of America is expanded into a global dream for mankind, and within that dream black America will find challenge, recognition, and support. The rendezvous with America is a rendezvous with self-realization for all the peoples of the world who have been excluded from the full democratic dream by poverty, class, or race" (*Plain Talk* 82).

Tolson's first book was, in general, well received. Robert Hilyer, writing in the *New York Times,* called the book an "admirable collection" (29). W. E. Garrison proclaimed: "This is a poetry which at once unveils some of the problems of our society and gives magnificent expression to the spirit of America as men of vision dare to hope that it really is" (1078). The mainstream African-American literary community was equally laudatory. Thus Langston Hughes writing from the pages of the *Chicago Defender* and P. L. Prattis for the *Pittsburgh Courier* both found much to admire in the book. Perhaps the most telling assessment would be written by Margaret Walker, an African-American poet and critic, in an essay entitled "New Adventures in Poetry." In a tone perfectly consistent with the assimilationist tendencies of the 1940s, Walker attempted to locate Tolson's work within the broader framework of American literary high art:

> It is thought provoking to such an extent that no one can honestly look upon this author and say here is another naive and simple Negro poet. *He is a poet to be reckoned with by all poets and one ventures to say that no better poetry has come out of America in recent years.* For those highly sensitive people who are tired of folk expression in Negro poetry, this work will come as a welcome boon; there is not one line of Negro dialect in the entire volume. One hopes and believes that in spite of its almost esoteric nature this book will find a wide mass audience as well. (n.p.)

In 1947 Tolson moved to Langston University in Langston, Oklahoma, no doubt lured by his former student Hobart Jarrett, who was now chair of the department of English. Here he met, among others, Oliver Cromwell Cox, author of *Class, Caste, and Race* (1948), an important book that challenged widely held notions about race and class. His years at Langston University proved to be crucial to his development as a mature poet and writer. The summer before he moved to Langston, Tolson was named poet laureate of the Liberian Centennial and Peace Exposition. As Farnsworth noted, "At any rate, this honor served to underscore the importance of Tolson's move from Wiley to Langston. It became not just a move from one school to another, but a passage from one stage of his career to another" (*Plain Talk* 108). The fruition of Tolson's connections with Liberia would be the 1953 publication of his *Libretto for the Republic of Liberia*. The poem, a long ode divided into eight parts corresponding to the sections of the diatonic scale, represented a considerable shift for Tolson with reference to poetic technique. Although thematically linked to *Rendezvous with America* in its emphasis on the ultimate progress of man through the eschewing of capitalism, colonial limitations, and its celebration of African cultural heritage (its locus was, of course, Liberia), the poem marked a significant change in direction. Tolson had had the manuscript read by Allen Tate, an active leader in the New Poetry movement who read the first draft with suggestions for fundamental change. The final product was a text written in the nonreferential modernist tradition (T. S. Eliot's *The Waste Land* is often cited as a model) replete with obscure historical allusions, quotations from other languages, and finally appended with a glossary designed to assist in the reader's process of decoding. The book received, in general, warm reviews from the bastions of American high culture. Writing in *The Nation,* John Ciardi remarked that "one feels a force of language and of rhythm as breathtaking as anything in the range of American poetry. This is obviously a book to return to. The blast of language and vision is simply too overwhelming for first judgments" (183). From the pages of the *New York Times Book Review,* Selden Rodman somewhat pontifically declared, "It is not only by all odds the most considerable poem so far written by an American Negro, but a work of poetic synthesis in the symbolic vein altogether worthy to be discussed in the company of such poems as 'The Wasteland,' 'The Bridge,' and 'Paterson'" (10). It was, however, Allen Tate's preface to the text proper that proved to be most telling. Tate wrote, "For the first time, it seems to me, a Negro poet has assimilated completely the full poetic language of his time and, by implication, the language of the Anglo-American poetic tradition" (11). While the white literary establishment generally seemed pleased and expressed their pleasure repeatedly by appropriating highly racialized discursive strategies, many senior African-American scholars were less impressed. Tolson's friend Langston Hughes, for example, wrote to his friend Arna Bontemps at the time of the book's publication, noting that Tolson had said that "he was going to write so many foreign words and footnotes that they would *have* to pay him some mind!" (Rampersad, Vol. II 235). It was, however, Jay Saunders Redding's review in the *Philadelphia Afro-American* that was most controversial. Redding took great exception with the obscurity of Tolson's language and thus praised in particular "the simplest lines, and the simplest lines are those that comprise the section titled Ti . . . which, Mr. Tate notwithstanding, find their inspiration in Dubois rather than Hart Crane" (n.p.). Redding's foregrounding of a specifically African-American referent is ironic given the fact that in 1959 in an address given at the First Congress of Negro Writers organized by the American Society of African culture, Redding rejected outright any claims for a distinctive culture for African Americans. According to Redding, not only was there no such thing as "American Negro literature," but it was so slight that to be seen it had to be pointed out.[1]

After the publication of the *Libretto,* Tolson continued to write, although his next book-length publication, *Harlem Gallery: Book I, The Curator* would not appear until 1965. In the intervening years, he wrote "The Negro Scholar" (*Midwest Journal* 1:1 [1948]: 80–82); "African China" (*Voices* 140 [Winter 1950]: 35–38); "E. & O. E." (*Poetry* 78:7 [1951]: 330–42, 369–72); "A Long Head to a Round Head" (*Beloit Poetry Journal* [1]:4 (1952): 19–21); and "The Man from Haliarnassus" (*Poetry* 81:1 [1952): 75–77). It would be *Harlem Gallery,* published one year before his death, that would anchor his reputation most firmly in the gallery of contemporary American letters. The book, without a doubt Tolson's most ambitious undertaking, was originally planned as a five-volume epic of the African-American experience. Similar to the *Libretto,* Tolson elected the odic mode and divided the long poem into twenty-four sections headed by the corresponding letters of the Greek alphabet. While its form was obviously informed by the canonical models of Western high art, its theme, "The odyssey of black American people" (*Plain Talk* 228), was highly inventive

1. See Tejumola Olaniyan, "African-American Critical Discourse and Invention of Cultural Identities." *African American Review* 26 (1992): 533–45.

and most particularly a product of African-American culture. Its critical reception, although in general quite positive, appears in many ways to be a replication of the ways in which the *Libretto* was read. Similar to the latter project, the book was buttressed by an introduction by a prominent member of the white intelligentsia (in this case Karl Shapiro), a practice that appears to have its roots in the tradition of the North American slave narratives, which were always prefaced by prominent white writers. Shapiro's comments were first published in the form of prepublication reviews, which appeared in *Book Week, The New York Herald Tribune,* and *The Washington Post* (*Plain Talk* 272). Here Shapiro declared with a self-assured prophetic tone that "a great poet has been living in our midst for decades and is almost totally unknown, even by the literati, even by poets" (11). Quite apart from the unqualified praise Shapiro had for *Harlem Gallery,* the review is probably best remembered for his assertion that "Tolson writes in Negro"(12). The statement at once problematized the notion that race was a determinant property of literary texts and showed to what a great extent institutional criticism such as anthologies and reviews in journals serve as paratexts that ultimately shape readers' attitudes about what they read. Critics such as Laurence Lieberman, Sarah Webster Fabio, and Gwendolyn Brooks all took exception to Shapiro's emphasis on "writing in Negro," which led to a curious critical obfuscation of the real value of the book that was theoretically under review. In spite of this, more balanced reviews appeared in *The London Times, Phylon,* and *The Saturday Review* that did much to promote Tolson as a major voice in contemporary American letters.

Recognition as a major poet came late for Tolson. He was sixty-seven at the time of the publication of *Harlem Gallery* and still teaching at Langston University. In the spring of 1965, he was offered the Avalon Chair in Humanities at The Tuskegee Institute where he taught for one semester. In 1966 Tolson received the American Academy of Arts and Letters Award in Literature. He still continued writing and had plans to complete the four other books of *Harlem Gallery,* when he died of cancer on August 29, 1966.

Tolson and His Critics

It is axiomatic that Melvin Tolson is a writer who, in comparison to his contemporaries, has been rather consistently overlooked. Michael Bérubé puts it this way: "Tolson has become our era's most neglected and undervalued modernist poet of consequence" (2–3). In a similar vein, James Payne wrote, "Melvin B. Tolson has remained a significantly undervalued American poetic talent" (110). While it is certainly true that in relation to writers such as Claude McKay, Jean Toomer, Countee Cullen, Langston Hughes, Arna Bontemps, Nella Larsen, and Zora Neal Hurston—all of whom have been traditionally viewed as constituting the core of the Harlem Renaissance—the work of Tolson has received far less critical attention, he has, nonetheless, been the object of serious recognition by scholars of African-American literature. In spite of the fact that two of his major books, *Libretto for the Republic of Liberia* (1953) and *Harlem Gallery* (1965) were prefaced and endorsed by major writers (Allen Tate and Karl Shapiro, respectively), it would not be until after his death in 1966 that he would begin to receive wider recognition by the academy. At the time of the writing of this essay, he has been the subject of no fewer than five book-length studies, six doctoral dissertations, and some twenty essays in scholarly journals. The editions of previously unpublished work edited by Robert Farnsworth (*A Gallery of Harlem Portraits* [1979] and *Caviar and Cabbage: Selected Columns by Melvin B. Tolson from the Washington Tribune* [1984] and Raymond Nelson's *"Harlem Gallery" and Other Poems of Melvin B. Tolson* [1999]) have done much to make his work more widely accessible. Tolson has also been the object of two biographies. The first, Joy Flasch's *Melvin B. Tolson* (1972), was based on Flasch's 1969 doctoral dissertation, "Melvin B. Tolson: A Critical Biography," done at Oklahoma State University, where Tolson had encouraged her to begin the project. The book offers a solid overview of his life and works up to the point of his death and attempts to explain the paradox of his relative obscurity in the context of American letters. In 1984, Robert Farnsworth published *Melvin B. Tolson 1898–1966: Plain Talk and Poetic Prophecy.* To date it is the most extensive critical work written on Tolson. Farnsworth's study, a meticulously researched biography of Tolson, was based on close readings of his primary texts, interviews with friends and family, and an examination of the Tolson papers in the Library of Congress. This allowed Farnsworth to determine the chronology of most of Tolson's writings, many of which were previously unknown. While Farnsworth's book is primarily descriptive, Mariann Russell's *Melvin B. Tolson's "Harlem Gallery": A Literary Analysis* (1980) was the first full-length critical study of Tolson's poetics. Here *Harlem Gallery* is studied primarily in relation to its rootings in African-American culture. Two full chapters are devoted to the Harlem of the 1930s. Russell was also the first to examine the connections between Tolson's early poems, *A Gallery of Portraits* and *Harlem Gallery.* According to Russell, Tolson's earlier poems served as a prototype for the more intellectually engaging work of his mature years, which was written in the modernist tradition similar in theme and technique to T. S. Eliot's *The Waste Land,* Ezra Pound's *Cantos,* and Hart Crane's *The Bridge.*

The most theoretical work on Tolson to date is Michael Bérubé's *Marginal Forces/Cultural Centers: Tolson, Pynchon, and the Politics of the Canon* (1992), which is based largely on Bérubé's 1989 doctoral dissertation. While Bérubé's goal is to contrast the critical receptions of the work of Tolson and the Anglo-American novelist Thomas Pynchon (1937–) in an effort to elucidate and challenge widely held notions regarding canonicity and author function, it is also a work of literary exegesis, since Bérubé devotes an entire chapter, "Tolson's Negativity: *Harlem Gallery* and the Idea of the Avant-Garde," to a close reading of Tolson's most widely regarded poem. In chapter 3, "Tolson's Neglect: African-American Modernism and Its Representations," Bérubé presents a reading of Tolson's reception history that underscores the importance of various forms of institutional criticism, including the function of the literary anthology in the shaping of an author's reputation. Bérubé's analysis of the role played by the anthologies of African-American poetry between the 1930s and 1960s in tandem with his exploration of the construction of a portrait of Tolson by the major scholars of contemporary African-American literature (namely Henry Louis Gates, Jr., and Houston Baker) contributed significantly to a serious re-evaluation of Tolson as a poet.

While not a formal study of Tolson's entire *oeuvre,* mention should be made of Raymond Nelson's edition, *"Harlem Gallery" and Other Poems* (1999). In addition to an insightful introduction by Rita Dove and the reprinting of "The Published Works of Melvin B. Tolson" from Farnsworth's *Plain Talk,* the book also contains meticulous explanatory notes to *Harlem Gallery.* Nelson's edition concludes with a 102-page section labeled "Notes and Commentary to Harlem Gallery." Nelson described the project in the following terms:

> The apparatus that follows should provide a reasonably well prepared and motivated reader a more or less comprehensive guide to what *Harlem Gallery* says and, step by step, what issues it raises. Only incidentally, as a tactic of accomplishing that primary goal, do I pay any particular attention to large patterns in the poem or global concerns of what it may mean. For each canto there is a narrative paraphrase of its action or discussion ("The Argument") and an annotation, as well as I can manage it, of the specific words, phrases, and ideas that require of the reader a knowledge that the poem itself does not provide. The annotations are keyed to line numbers. (367)

The Odyssey of a Thesis

While critics have studied Tolson's poetry and his role as a social commentator, his position as a literary critic has received little attention. Tolson lived in Harlem during the 1931–32 academic year while he worked on his master's degree under the auspices of a Rockefeller grant. There was even some early confusion over the dates of his stay in Harlem. While Joy Flasch indicates that Tolson finished his studies at Columbia in 1931, other evidence suggests that he spent the academic year 1931–32 in New York. In his essay, "The Odyssey of a Manuscript," Tolson clearly indicates that in 1932 he was a graduate student in an eastern university. Confusion over the date of his residence in Harlem was no doubt caused in part by Tolson himself. For example, in an interview with M. W. King on March 10, 1965, entitled "A Poet's Odyssey," he gave 1930 as the beginning date of his Rockefeller fellowship.

> In 1930, I was a student, on Rockefeller fellowship at Columbia University. . . . The thesis for my degree was called "The Harlem Group of Negro Writers." As you know, the Twenties gave birth not only to the Lost Generation, but to the Harlem Renaissance and the New Negro. Jazz became a fad—ancient African art, a novelty of the intelligentsia. ("A Poet's Odyssey" 194)

Tolson's dissertation was directed by Edward Arthur Christy (1899–1946), who is acknowledged in the preface. During the academic year 1931–32 Christy would have been a mere thirty-two years of age, a virtual contemporary of Tolson's. He was also a Columbia graduate. His doctoral dissertation, "The Orient in American Transcendentalism: A Study of Emerson, Thoreau, and Alcott," was completed in 1932. Christy was an early comparativist and, by today's standards, no doubt would be considered a multiculturalist. He was an independent thinker as noted by a comment in the preface to his dissertation, which was published by the Columbia University Press:

> Finally, I should state that since this book was undertaken upon my own initiative; worked out largely according to my own ideas, I am solely responsible for its conclusions; those members of the faculties of Columbia University whom I have the honor to acknowledge as masters must in no way be blamed for my indiscretions. (Christy VI)

Mariann Russell recognized the influence of Christy on Tolson's work: "The notion of 'The world's cultural fabric,' the interrelatedness of various cultures, came to Tolson through Arthur Christy, a favorite teacher at Columbia" (7). In fact, so profound was Tolson's gratitude toward his former teacher that he recognized his former mentor in a note that accompanied the text of *Libretto for the Republic of Liberia*. In Christy, Tolson had obviously found a mentor and a critic who was willing to break with tradition. After all, in the 1930s to have written on living authors, let alone African-American authors, was virtually unheard of. The prevailing literary model of the day perhaps was most appropriately summarized in T.S. Eliot's observations, "What Is a Classic?": A classic stands out only in retrospect and contemporary evaluations—given their emotional proximity—usually fail to recognize it. To study a literary movement contemporary with its moment of creation, in fact, was a major departure from the dominant critical notions of the era. While it is true that philological and biographical criticism were still the prevailing theoretical modes used in American and British universities in the 1920s, by the late 1920s and early 1930s the impact of the New Criticism was becoming evident in most institutions of higher learning. Rejecting the impressionistic commentary and unsupported evaluations that had characterized earlier biobibliographical criticism, the New Criticism sought to develop a more systematic system for the analysis of texts. Tolson's approach, however, was far closer to traditional biographical criticism, for he was, after all, historicizing a movement contemporary with its moment of creation.

Although Tolson worked on his dissertation during his fellowship year, it was not formally submitted until 1940. The long period from initiation to final completion can be explained in part by the fact that Tolson was a full-time faculty member at Wiley College in addition to being a debate coach. More important, however, was his role as a creative writer. In addition to the writing of *Gallery of Harlem Portraits,* Tolson, who wrote a number of plays and had begun to work on a novel in the late 1930s, was also writing a weekly column for the *Washington Tribune* entitled "Caviar and Cabbage."

His papers, for example, contain a letter from the William Morris Agency dated November 6, 1930, indicating receipt of his play, *Southern Front.* By November 10, the play had already been read, and Robert Goodhue wrote to Tolson, inviting him to let the agency represent him. Tolson agreed to the arrangement, although there is no further indication that the Morris Agency actually succeeded in placing the play. At the same time, Tolson apparently was involved in the writing of a novel entitled *All Aboard.* As late as October 17, 1939, his close friend V. F. Calverton wrote to him chiding him for not completing the book:

> Dear MB:
>
> Things have been moving fast and furious of late, and it has been impossible for me to answer any mail, not even your sweet, affectionate letters. As I did write you, I am very happy about your getting that scholarship. How much does it actually mean in money, and what are you going to do about it? A letter from Andy indicates you haven't done a lot of writing yet. For Christ's sake, MB, write that novel, won't you, and stop talking about it. If you would shut up your trap a bit and tie yourself up to a chair and typewriter, you would get something done, something really worthwhile and significant. (Tolson Papers)

Tolson scholars have conjectured about the awarding of the degree. Mariann Russell wrote the following:

> According to rumor at Wiley College, the reason for the delay in the awarding of Tolson's degree was that instead of studying at Columbia he was walking the streets of Harlem. This apocryphal story may have been based on Tolson's descriptions of the particularities of the Harlem he observed and in which he participated. (6)

In a letter from one of his former students, Hobart Jarrett, to Richard Farnsworth dated June 14, 1982, Jarrett alludes to the fact that some of Tolson's jealous colleagues at Wiley had apparently created the fiction that Tolson never received his degree at all (Tolson Papers). Farnsworth guessed that the delay was due to the fact that "Tolson never placed much importance on titles and degrees, he carelessly took no interest in making the revisions and applying for the degree until many years later when the Wiley administration began to be increasingly concerned about the college's accreditation" (*Plain Talk* 40).

A more plausible explanation may have to do with Tolson's self-image as a writer and the way he approached all forms of writing. He preferred, by his own admission, to work simultaneously on several projects at once and harbored unrealistic expectations about what he might likely accomplish. In an application for a fellowship from the Rosenwald foundation most probably submitted in 1948, Tolson specifically addressed these issues. He wrote:

> I seem to get the best results when I'm writing both prose and poetry—that is, going from one to the other, one stimulating the other, one recuperating me for the other. I thought this a little strange until I picked up the other day *The Art of Writing Fiction,* by Mary Burchard Orvis, who said, "The best writing is that which conveys the poetic quality." So, while working on the novel *All Aboard,* I completed the long poem for the Republic of Liberia and finished the dramatization of George Schuyler's novel *Black No More.*
>
> During the tenure of the fellowship I intend to finish *All Aboard* and the epic *A Gallery of Harlem Portraits* and begin the tetralogy covering four generations of Negroes in Africa and the New World. . . .
>
> During the two-year tenure of the fellowship I shall revise the epic *A Gallery of Harlem Portaits*—parts of which appeared in the *Modern Quarterly* and the *Arts Quarterly.* It is a poem similar to Masters' *Spoon River Anthology,* with Harlem as a magnet drawing characters of diversified types from all corners of the world. It gives, I trust, Negro America, [*sic*] its comedy and tragedy, in prismatic epitome.
>
> This poetic revision will go along with my completion of *All Aboard* and the work on the first volume of the tetralogy, which is laid in Africa and deals with the slave trade and the Middle Passage. In writing the Liberian poem a great amount of research in African origins was done; so these data will be useful in this initial novel.

> A writer who tries to give a plan for a novel or a poem is probably a hypocrite. No writer can tell just how a creation will work out. If an artist has intellectual integrity, he starts with an inspiration and ends in perspiration, with a supplication. (Tolson Papers)

It seems reasonable to assume that Tolson wrote the initial draft of his thesis while living in New York. It is apparent, however, that he did do some writing after he left Harlem. There is, as Farnsworth notes, a footnote to an interview with Harriet Monroe in the spring of 1934. Further, his interview with Zona Gale most probably took place on Thanksgiving Day, 1932 (*Plain Talk* 40). Also, there are multiple references to Harlan Hatcher's *Creating the American Novel,* which was not published until 1935. The conclusion, which brings Tolson's study to a close, quotes from an editorial published in *New Challenge: A Literary Quarterly* in the fall of 1937—some five years after Tolson had returned to Texas.

"The Harlem Group": Mapping Out the Renaissance

Very little has been written on Tolson's thesis. This apparent critical omission may be explained, in part, by its status as a published work. Unlike many of the assessments of the period, which began to appear as early as the late 1930s in books such as Benjamin Brawley's *The Negro Genius* (1937), Tolson's thesis remained largely invisible. It was after all not a printed book, and in the absence of a bibliographic citation system that would call attention to its existence, it would have to await the recovery project initiated by Tolson's critics that began only after his death in 1966. Joy Flasch limits her comments to a description of the contents of the thesis, while Jon Woodson in a 1986 essay merely questioned Tolson's choice of the writers he studied: "The work, 'The Harlem Group of Negro Writers,' encompassed only those individuals Tolson personally knew, though this is a somewhat curious restriction as the thesis is composed of plot outlines and paraphrases of reviews and does not reflect Tolson's personal acquaintance with the Harlem writers" (22). Michael Bérubé's only reference to the thesis is in a footnote in which he refers to Tolson's residence in Harlem during 1931–32 and the genesis of *A Gallery of Harlem Portraits:*

> The Harlem Renaissance had special significance for Tolson, not only in that it was the central African-American cultural configuration of the first half of the century but, more specifically, in that Tolson lived briefly in New York during 1931–32, on a fellowship at Columbia, writing an M.A. thesis titled "The Harlem Group of Negro Writers." At no other point in his life, certainly, was he as near the epicenter of a movement as he was during his year at Columbia. In fact, the mustard seed from which *Harlem Gallery* eventually sprouted was apparently a sonnet composed during that year. (105)

Tolson's biographer, Richard Farnsworth, supplies the most complete information concerning Tolson's residence in Harlem as well as the most extensive commentary on the thesis as well. Given its importance, I quote it at length:

> Harlem had already fascinated and charged the imaginations of a generation of writers, many of whom, like Langston Hughes, were Tolson's contemporaries. Tolson's M.A. thesis, "The Harlem Group of Negro Writers," is his earliest written comment on these writers. He almost certainly was aware of their work prior to this time, but the thesis is a very deliberate effort to identify and summarize the importance of their work as a group, both to fulfill an academic requirement and, more importantly, to examine their usefulness as precursors to his own writing career. It is from this point on that Tolson's own work warrants serious critical attention.
>
> Reflecting the strong influence of Alain Locke, Tolson in his thesis emphasized Harlem's role as a cosmopolitan city within a cosmopolitan city, a city that engendered a "New Negro," a cosmopolitan Negro, different from the antebellum and postbellum stereotypes of the past.
>
> Tolson treated the Harlem Renaissance itself as a "phase of the postwar development in American literature." World War I, the cosmopolitanism of New York City, and interest and support of white patrons and writers—and particularly of publishing companies—the exciting and ambitious appearance of *Fire* and *Harlem,* the sustaining support of the NAACP and the Urban League, and the growing research in Negro history are all briefly discussed as important contributing factors to the Renaissance.
>
> Tolson then devoted individual chapters to Countee Cullen, Langston Hughes, Claude McKay, Walter White, Eric Walrond, Rudolph Fisher, Jessie Fauset, George Schuyler, W.E.B. Du Bois, James Weldon Johnson,

> and Wallace Thurman. A revealing grouping, perhaps a little heavy on writer-leaders. Notable ommissions are Jean Toomer, Arna Bontemps, and Sterling Brown. Zora Neale Hurston is referred to in the conclusion as on of "the new school" of writers succeeding the Renaissance. Marcus Garvey and his movement are virtually ignored. Alain Locke is quoted frequently as the philosophical spokesman for the Renaissance. (*Plain Talk* 34)

Farnsworth was particularly interested in Tolson's discussion of George S. Schuyler and Langston Hughes—two writers with whom Tolson identified personally and who had an impact on his own work. One of the few critics to identify the importance of Tolson's thesis in relation to his development as a poet and thinker was Craig Hansen Werner. He noted that early in his writing career:

> Tolson's explicit awareness of both the oral and visual aesthetics provided a nearly unique foundation for his search for a synthetic sensibility. His M.A. thesis, "The Harlem Group of Negro Writers," identifies Hughes's adaptation of Afro-American music to mainstream American prosody as a significant aesthetic development. At the same time, Tolson was developing his interest in visual aesthetics in the sections of Harlem portraits titled "Chiaroscuros," "Silhouettes," "Etchings," and "Pastels" in *A Gallery of Harlem Portraits*. (166)

Writing on the Harlem Renaissance today might seem a task akin to bringing coals to Newcastle. After all, some seventy years after its theoretical demise, so much has been written on both the period and its participants that the sheer bulk of writing would daunt the most voracious reader. Then, too, there is the problem of attempting to historicize a period in American literature so deeply embedded in a series of polemics largely related to questions of race and canonicity. A. Yemisi Jimoh in a review of *The Harlem Renaissance, 1920–1940: Vol. 5—Remembering the Harlem Renaissance* put it this way: "Almost everything about the period in African American literature that is typically termed the Harlem Renaissance has been contested. The name, the location, the dates for the era, whether or not it was a 'renaissance,' as well as the event itself—all have come under question at some point" (526).

Where, then, does Tolson's early work—a study written from an unusual temporal and emotive proximity to the object of its inquiry—relate to a generalized taxonomy of renaissance studies? I would argue that to understand Tolson's reading of the renaissance one must look both at this organizational frame and at how he to chose to incorporate his sources. Tolson's first chapter, "A Perspective of Harlem" is prefaced by quotations from five poets, four black (Countee Cullen, Paul Laurence Dunbar, Langston Hughes, Fenton Johnson) and one white (Walt Whitman). These poetic epigraphs convey a voice and a perspective that prefigures the attitude toward race and class that will be a thematic constant in Tolson's thesis. As Mariann Russell noted, "The lines from the black poets stressed different responses to the black man's desire to 'sing,' from the dilemma of Cullen . . . to the exaltation of Fenton Johnson . . . Tolson recognized the possibility of the creation of an ethnic literature and saw a Whitmanesque value in its creation" (40–41). While this is certainly true, Tolson was also most definitely celebrating both the history and diversity of African-American poetry since the poets cited range from Paul Laurence Dunbar (1872–1906), the most popular African-American poet of the turn of the century, to the relatively unknown Fenton Johnson (1888–1958), who is most remembered for stark depictions of urban despair. The only poem quoted in full is Langston Hughes's "Aesthete in Harlem," which was first published in *Opportunity* in June 1930—a poem in which, according to Arnold Rampersad, "Hughes wrote of searching, estrangement, and ironic discovery" (Vol. I 188). The "nigger place," of course, was Harlem, and it was, after all, Harlem and its black voices that were at the center of Tolson's project.

Tolson's decisions about which authors to include in his thesis is an issue that should be addressed because any process of selection implies the tacit construction of a canon. Since the notion of a Harlem Renaissance first emerged, the list of "central figures" has been a matter of constant renegotiation. The desire for generic representation, no doubt, accounts for some of Tolson's choices. Tolson wrote that among his goals was to "emphasize the lives and works of *the leading* (emphasis mine) contemporary Negro essayists, short story writers, novelists, and poets in the light of modern criticism" (4). Farnsworth finds the grouping "perhaps a little heavy on writer-leaders" (*Plain Talk* 34) and laments the omissions of Jean Toomer, Arna Bontemps, and Sterling Brown. Since there is no master list of representative renaissance writers against which to measure Tolson's choices, all arguments in favor of inclusion or exclusion are open to debate. Not only have the dates that frame the renaissance been subject to constant renegotiations but so has the list of central figures. Roger Whitlow, in *Black American Literature: A Critical History* (1974) includes nine writers: Alain Locke, Claude McKay, Jean Toomer, Countee Cullen, Langston Hughes, Nella Larsen, George S. Schuyler, Arna Bontemps, and Zora Neale Hurston, while Roger M. Valade, III, in *The Essential Black Literature Guide* (1994), considers "the major writers" to be Claude McKay, Jean Toomer, Countee Cullen, Lanston Hughes, Arna Bontemps, Nella Larsen, and Zora Neale Hurston—a reduction of two from Whitlow's canon. Steven Watson, in *The Harlem Renaissance: Hub of African-American Culture, 1920–1930,* appears to be even more selective. Among its "best known figures" he includes only Hughes, Hurston, Cullen, McKay, and Toomer. Tolson's early canon of eleven participants seems to have been subjected to a narrowing process. It is telling that Tolson continued to review his concept of the renaissance and the writers who consitutued its core well to the end of his career. In a set of "Key Words in *Harlem Gallery,*" dated 1966, he wrote the following:

> *Harlem Renaissance:*
>
> A real movement in Harlem during the '20s. By the way, I did my thesis at Columbia College on this. Dr. Alain Locke, Howard University philosopher, published *The New Negro.* For the frist time Negro intellectuals en masse discorded [*sic*] the Tuskegee Sage—the Booker T. Washington of the Horatio-Alger philosophy. The Talented Tenth of Dr. W.E.B. Du Bois took over. Answering the race riots of 1919, Claude McKay, the Jamaican poet whom Winston Churchill later quoted in the House of Commons after Dunkirk, published the sonnet "If We Must Die," which echoed across the country. The poem was denounced by conservative whites as evidence of a new spirit among Negroes. Senator Cabot Lodge read it into the records of Congress. Paul Lawrence Dunbar, the Negro dialect poet, was replaced by a galaxy that included Langston Hughes, Countee Cullen, Sterling Brown, James Weldon Johnson, Jean Toomer, Arna Bontemps. Novelists appeared: Fessie [*sic*] Fauset, Claude McKay, Nella Larsen, Arna Bontemps, Rudolph Fisher, W.E.B. Du Bois. W. C. Handy, King Oliver, Jelly Roll Morton, Louis Armstrong and others came out of New Orleans, Memphis, Kansas City, Chicago, and Chicago [*sic*], with a "new song"—the Blues, Jazz. (Tolson Papers)

Tolson's list of central writers of the renaissance clearly reflects a bias in favor of writers who were productive at the time Tolson had begun to conceptualize his project. With the exception of Du Bois who was already an established writer in the 1930s (he would have been sixty-three in 1931), most of the writers were in their late twenties to mid-thirties and at the peak of their creative powers. The only female writer included was Jessie Fauset (1882–1961), the editorial assistant to W.E.B. Du Bois at *The Crisis*, who had been responsible for nurturing many of the younger poets such as Langston Hughes. Perhaps most important to Tolson's decision to include or exclude writers from his "Harlem Group" was the fact that by the time he began to write his thesis he was clearly dependent on written sources to validate his own judgments. Thus Tolson's construction of a fixed, representative group was radically contingent on choices that had already been made by the slightly older generation of writers and scholars. It was logical then that he would depend heavily on the earlier work of Alain Locke (1886–1954), who had edited the seminal anthology *The New Negro* in 1925. Locke's anthology—an impressive collection of poetry and prose by and about African Americans and buttressed by an extensive bibliography—appeared but six years prior to Tolson's arrival in Harlem.[2] The anthology was based on the March 1925 issue of *Survey Graphic*, entitled "Harlem—Mecca of the New Negro." Considering that the initial print run of 30,000 copies was followed by a second edition of 12,000 copies (Long 16), it would not be surprising that Tolson had read the first version in Texas, well before his fellowship year. In fact, with the exception of George Schuyler and Walter White, *all* of the writers included in Tolson's canon first appeared in the *New Negro*.

Tolson also incorporated into his thesis ideas and concepts that had been previously elaborated on by other scholars. For example, the antithetical nature of the poetry of Countee Cullen and Langston Hughes was pointed out by Elizabeth Lay Green in *The Negro in Contemporary Literature: An Outline for Individual and Group Study* (1928) as well as by James Weldon Johnson in his 1931 revision of *The Book of American Negro Poetry*. Green, the wife of Paul Green, the Pulitzer Prize winning playwright who had written

2. For an excellent discussion of Locke's anthology, see Arnold Rampersad's introduction to *The New Negro Edited by Alain Locke*. New York: Simon and Schuster, 1997.

plays depicting African-American rural life such as *In Abraham's Bosom,* was the first to refer to Hughes as "a rebel"—an idea that James Weldon Johnson expanded upon in his classic anthology. Tolson was familiar with both sources and recast the formulation in his chapter on Hughes.

Because Tolson's study appeared some thirty years prior to the publication of the first major retrospective histories of the renaissance years—Nathan Huggins's *Harlem Renaissance* (1971), David Levering Lewis's *When Harlem Was in Vogue* (1981), and Jervis Anderson's *This Was Harlem: A Cultural Portrait* (1982)—it has a paradigmatic relationship to these later books, most specifically in relation to the way Tolson elected to create a historiographic map of the renaissance years. Tolson's first two chapters, "A Perspective of Harlem" and "The Negro or Harlem Renaissance" (the first a history of Harlem, the second a discussion of the cultural and institutional forces that shaped the renaissance) are virtually replicated by all future literary historians. The parameters of the period vary slightly. While Tolson and Anderson use 1917 as a point of origin, Huggins and Lewis elect the 1919 triumphant return from the war of the black Fifteenth Regiment. The undergirding principle, that is, the use of fixed historical moments, remains the same. Tolson assigned no specific date to the end of the renaissance, choosing instead to reference an editorial in *New Challenge,* a journal founded by Dorothy West (1909–). Here the editors refer to the renaissance "which grew steadily and upon false foundations ten years ago" (3). Since the editorial was published in the fall of 1937, that would place the end of the renaissance in the mid-1920s. It is clear from his dating of the movement that Tolson was still conceptualizing his project some five years after he left Columbia University. Huggins, echoing Langston Hughes, refers to the 1929 stock market crash. Lewis selects the 1935 race riot in Harlem, and Anderson extends his study until the early 1950s. Tolson's decision to preface his study proper with a discussion, albeit brief, of the significant role played by the complex set of interlocking forces such as the influence of editors, white patrons, and African-American cultural institutions (e.g., the role of the National Association for the Advancement of Colored People and its official publication, *The Crisis*), all become central topics in future studies of the Renaissance.

Tolson's thesis was, of course, a product of its times. Written during the Depression and in the context of a deeply segregated society, it is a text that reflects the tensions of those times. One of the most remarkable features of this early study of a key moment of cultural change is Tolson's role as mediator between the white literary establishment and the world of African-American letters and scholarship, which is reflected in his use of sources. In his first chapter, "The History of Harlem," Tolson carefully elected to bracket the concept of race. Race for Tolson's purpose would not become a substantive essence but rather a conceptual and social schema. He thus wrote, "In this thesis the term Negro will be used in its sociological sense" (10). To undergird his position, he then quoted from Melville J. Herskovits's *The American Negro* (1928). Tolson's decision to cite Herskovits (1895–1963) is hardly surprising. Herskovits, after all, was a towering presence in African-American intellectual life during the first half of the twentieth century. In the field of anthropology, he single-handedly addressed the major topics of the research agenda, which had been drawn up by his own mentor, Franz Boas, an important influence on writers during the Harlem Renaissance. Herskovits, like Arthur Christy, was also a Columbia graduate, having received a Ph.D. in 1923. Although Herskovits's major book, *The Myth of the Negro Past* (1941), did not appear until one year after Tolson had completed his thesis, he was an influential figure in renaissance circles during the 1920s. As George Hutchinson aptly noted: "The cultural 'naissance' happens to match the current process of formation of a 'veritable new Negro, the American Negro' as an indigenous physical type. Herskovits' work connects the New Negro movement, American cultural nationalism, and Boasian anthropology" (75). While the book from which Tolson quotes, *The American Negro,* was not published until 1928, Herskovits had already been a contributor to the famous March 1925 issue of *The Survey Graphic,* a source that is cited frequently in his thesis. Herskovits's "The Dilemma of Social Pattern," which appeared here for the first time, was later revised and included in Alain Locke's *The New Negro.* It was an essay that stressed assimilation and "complete acculturation" of African Americans. By drawing parallels between the state of African-American culture and those of other marginalized groups (he specifically refers to American Jews), Herskovits was clearly evoking an encoded belief that American culture constituted a melting pot. Although his views of ethnic assimilation clearly did not involve intermarrriage, nonetheless his discourse was marshaled to create a sense of national unity and cultural cohesion so essential to the American dream.

Herskovits's centrist position, which allows for features of cultural distinctiveness within a majority culture and yet appeals on another level to a sense of nation building, would no doubt have been particularly appealing to Tolson, who would, in his first book *Rendezvous with America,* make the same appeal. Although *The American Negro* represented an early stage in Herskovits's intellectual development, which emphasized the study of physical types, later he would place much greater emphasis upon the retrieval of the past in which he would stress the ultimate African origin of New World diasporic culture.

Tolson continued to follow the career of Herskovits. In a set of typed notes entitled "Key Words in *Harlem Gallery,*" which appear in the Tolson papers, he specifically refers to Herskovits. The note, which is keyed to page two of the manuscript, reads as follows:

> *The Myth of the Afro-American Past:*
>
> Melville J. Herskovits, Director, Professor of American Studies, Northwestern U., spent a lifetime researching African lore and folkways. He attempted to explain the complexities of African cultures brought to America. Contrast this with Gertrude Stein's remark to Paul Robeson in Paris (see page 56): 'The Negro suffers from nothingness' because [*sic*] of the contempt of white people for the word *Negro* and their downgrading of the African heritage, a movement was launched at the famous bookstore at 125th St. and 7th Ave. in Harlem to change the word *Negro* to *Afro-American.* Jacob Drachler has just edited a significant book, *African Heritage,* with a preface by Herskovits, just before he died. The articles are by African, European and American writers. Excerpts from *My Libretto for the Republic of Liberia* are used as Prologue, Interlude, and Epilogue. (Tolson Papers)

Another telling feature of Tolson's thesis was his use of the major anthologies of African-American literature published during the 1920s. It would not be unfair to say that a history of the Harlem Renaissance is a history of key period anthologies.[3] Prior to the 1920s—the period roughly

---

3. For a discussion of the role played by special-interest anthologies during the Harlem Renaissance period, see my study *Afro-Cuban Literature: Critical Junctures.* Westport, CT: Greenwood, 1998. 149–64.

corresponding to the Harlem Renaissance—African-American writers were virtually unknown to the American public. While it is true that E. C. Stedman, one of the most respected critics of the late nineteenth century, did include a few poems by Paul Laurence Dunbar (1872–1906) in his massive *American Anthology* (1900), the poems reprinted (dialect verse) reflected and reinforced long-standing racial stereotypes. The cultural climate of the 1920s was far more receptive to cultural dialogue, and no fewer than six collections of African-American poetry were published in the twenties: James Weldon Johnson's *The Book of American Negro Poetry* (1922, 1931), Robert T. Kerlin's *Negro Poets and Their Poems* (1923), Newman Ivey White's *An Anthology of Verse by American Negroes* (1924), Alain Locke's *The New Negro* (1925), Countee Cullen's *Caroling Dusk* (1927), and V. F. Calverton's *An Anthology of American Negro Literature* (1929). Although two anthologies edited by African-Americans appeared in the 1930s (Robert B. Eleazer's *Singers in the Dawn: A Brief Anthology of American Negro Poetry* [1934] and Beatrice M. Murphy's *An Anthology of Contemporary Verse: Negro Voices* [1938]), it would not be until the publication of the *Negro Caravan: Writings by American Negroes* (1941), which was edited by Sterling A. Brown and Arthur P. Davis, and the *Poetry of the Negro* (1949), a compilation of two renaissance poets, Arna Bontemps and Langston Hughes, that works by African Americans would be again subject to a serious project of preservation.

While quite different from their European counterparts, the North American anthologists of the 1920s elected to include only poetry written by blacks—a decision mirrored by Tolson in his study of the renaissance. Their projects taken as a whole shows that African-American culture was neither monolithic nor overstructured. Ideas and concepts about race and literary axiology appear to have been in a state of flux and renegotiation. While James Weldon Johnson sought to valorize black culture, Newman Ivey White tried to appropriate what he felt to be acceptable for the larger canon of North American literature. African-American literary artifacts then became part of a larger socio-political project. It was Countee Cullen, with his own tortured ambivalence about his own sense of (black) selfness, who would touch, albeit unintentionally, on one of the fundamental problematics of the time. What cannot be overlooked is that these important anthologies, in spite of their conflicting principles of organization, were clear gestures toward a pluralism and were intended to open the canon.

With the exception of White's *An Anthology of Verse by American Negroes* (Tolson probably could not tolerate the editor's condescending attitude toward blacks) all the other works were cited. James Weldon Johnson's 1931 edition of *The Book of American Negro Poetry* was cited most frequently (twelve times) followed by V. F. Calverton's *Anthology of American Negro Poetry* with eleven references. Cullen's *Caroling Dusk* was referenced ten times while Alain Locke's *The New Negro* was used only five times, and Kerlin's *Negro Poets and Their Poems* appears but once. Tolson's familiarity with these books is not only a good gauge of how current he was with the scholarship of the time, but shows his sensitivity to the overall importance of the special interest anthology and its role in the shaping of the canon. There seems to be a consensus that although there is no fixed sequence in canon formation, certain general principles—(1) preservation, (2) nationalism and historicizing, (3) the belief in transhistorical excellence, and (4) revisionism as a response to the established canon—chart more or less accurately the stages through which anthologists have traditionally moved (Golding 279–84). The process is most clearly seen at the opposite ends of the spectrum: preservation symbolized in the great books curriculum, which views selected texts from earlier periods at the cornerstones of Western civilization, in contrast to revisionists, who view the voices rarely heard as the most authentic expressions of contemporary culture. Tolson's project was linked to the last stage of this grid.

In many ways, Tolson's thesis played a role somewhat analogous to the early poetic vignettes of the *Gallery of Harlem Poets,* serving as a prototype for a more mature critical discourse. But there were some constants that link his work across time. In writing his thesis, Tolson created an intellectual mosaic in which he juxtaposed diverse critical and aesthetic sensibilities to construct a period history of African-American writing that reflected his beliefs in what he considered universal art and expression. Harlem for Tolson was not only the epicenter of writing by and about blacks, but formed part of a larger national cultural fabric. As an African American writing from the context of a deeply segregated society, he used writing as a means of bridging a wide cultural divide. To resolve this split, he deliberately drew on the intellectual resources from both the African-American community and the majority culture. His use of primary and secondary source materials is a clear gesture toward cultural pluralism. Thus, next to the bastions of middle-class American culture, *The Nation, Book-*

man, The Saturday Review of Literature, Survey, American Mercury, and *Poetry,* stand citations to the premier organs of high black culture: *The Crisis, Opportunity, Negro World, New Challenge,* and *Harlem.*

By and large, the critics to whom he turned as authorities were by the late 1920s respected members of the American cultural community. James Weldon Johnson, the writer most frequently cited was, no doubt, the most widely known African-American writer of the time. He served as an important model for Tolson, since Johnson was keenly aware of the pitfalls of the racial divide and had addressed the issue in "The Dilemma of the Negro Author," published in December 1928 in *American Mercury.* The other African-American writers whom he cited with some frequency (Countee Cullen, Alain Locke) were used as voices of authority based largely on the important work that they had done in the field of literary and cultural recovery. For more basic information, Tolson turned to the standard texts about African-American culture and life. As one might expect, these authors, such as Scott Nearing (1883–1982), Mary White Ovington (1865–1951), and Victor Francis Calverton (1900–1940), were by and large social reformers and members of the intellectual left. Calverton, the socialist writer and editor of *Modern Quarterly,* had in fact been the first to publish some of Tolson's poetry. He became one of his closest friends and served as an entrée into the cultural world of the Bohemian left. Calverton's views on the importance of African-American writing were clearly congruent with Tolson's own beliefs, since echoing the earlier formulation of Van Wyck Brooks's *America's Coming-of-Age,* he felt that the only original literary expression in the United States must be black-based, for it was the only form that could be used as an authentic alternative to European cultural imperialism. Calverton's writings (*The Liberation of American Literature,* 1932, is a case in point) may be legitimately read as a discourse on U.S. cultural identity, one that addresses basic issue of race and national literary consciousness. The same nation-building agenda also informed one of Tolson's other sources, Russell Blankenship's *American Literature as an Expression of the National Mind* (1931), which he cited at least five times. In spite of Blankenship's racialist views (he felt that African blood shaped "the humor of the race . . . the quickly changeable emotional temper" [44]), Tolson used him as a source for factual information on Harlem and quoted his opinions on Cullen and Hughes. Far less problematic was Harlan Hatcher's *Creating the Modern American Novel* (1935) and Alfred Kreymborg's *Our Singing Strength* (1929), since both authors had a clearly more sympathetic position toward the emerging canon of black writing.

It is a paradox that Tolson, one of the earliest African-American writers to study the renaissance is conspicuously absent from virtually every major study of the movement. Nathan Huggins does refer to him in *The Harlem Renaissance* but groups him with "recent writers" such as Saul Bellow and Ralph Ellison. George Hutchinson in *The Harlem Renaissance in Black and White* places him in a next generation of writers who demonstrate continuities between renaissance networks and writing in the 1930s. The emphasis in both cases is on Tolson's poetry, which, in fact, did not achieve much recognition until the watershed years of the renaissance had long passed. In spite of the fact that his reputation as a poet has tended to diminish his role as a critic, a study of "The Harlem Group of Negro Writers" reveals another important dimension of Tolson's persona. For much like his poetry, in which he consistently sought to harmonize the diverse cultural codes of America, in "The Harlem Group" Tolson succeeded in capturing both the optimism and tensions congruent with, but integral to, a moment of nodal change in American culture and society.

Works Cited

Bérubé, Michael. *Marginal Forces/Cultural Centers: Tolson, Pynchon and the Politics of the Canon*. Ithaca and London: Cornell UP, 1992.

Blankenship, Russell. *American Literature as an Expression of the National Mind*. New York: H. Holt and Co., 1931.

Christy, Edward Arthur. *The Orient in AmericanTranscendentalism: A Study of Emerson, Thoreau and Alcott*. New York: Octagon Books, 1960.

Ciardi, John. "Recent Verse." *The Nation* 178.7 (27 February 1954): 183.

"Editorial." *New Challenge: A Literary Quarterly* 2 (Fall 1937): 3–4.

Farnsworth, Robert M. *Melvin B. Tolson 1898–1966: Plain Talk and Poetic Prophesy*. Columbia: U of Missouri P, 1984.

Garrison, W. E. "Books in Brief." *The Christian Century* 61.38 (20 September 1944): 1078–79.

Golding, Alan C. "A History of American Poetry Anthologies." *Canons* Ed. Robert von Halberg. Chicago: U of Chicago P, 1983. 279–307.

Hilyer, Robert. "Among the New Volumes of Verse." *New York Times Book Review* (10 December 1944): 29.

Hutchinson, George. *The Harlem Renaissance in Black and White*. Cambridge and London: Harvard UP, 1995.

Jimoh, A. Yemisi. "Review of Cary D. Wintz, *The Harlem Renaissance, 1920–1940.*" *African American Review* 33 (1999): 526–28.

Long, Richard. "The Genesis of Locke's *The New Negro.*" *Black World* 25.4 (1976): 15–20.

Melvin Beaunorus Tolson: A *Register of His Papers in the Library of Congress.* Prepared by C. L. Craig (1976) and David Mathisen (1984), revised and expanded by Nan Thompson Ernst. Washington, D. C.: Manuscript Division of the Library of Congress, 1997.

Nelson, Raymond, ed. *"Harlem Gallery" and Other Poems of Melvin B. Tolson.* Charlottesville and London: UP of Virginia, 1999.

Payne, James. "Review of *A Gallery of Harlem Portraits.*" *World Literature Today* 57 (1983): 110.

Rampersad, Arnold. *The Life of Langston Hughes, Vol. I: 1902–1941: I, Too, Sing America.* New York, Oxford: Oxford UP, 1986.

———. *The Life of Langston Huges, Vol. II: 1941–1967: I Dream a World.* New York, Oxford: Oxford UP, 1988.

Redding, J. Saunders. "Book Review." *Philadelphia Afro-American* (23 January 1954): n.p.

Rodman, Selden. "On Vistas Undreamt." *New York Times Book Review* (24 January 1954): 10.

Russell, Mariann. *Melvin B. Tolson's "Harlem Gallery": A Literary Analysis.* Columbia and London: U of Missouri P, 1980.

Shapiro, Karl. "Introduction" in *Harlem Gallery: Book I, The Curator* by Melvin B. Tolson. New York: Twayne, 1965.

Tate, Allen. "Preface" in *Libretto for the Republic of Liberia* by Melvin B. Tolson. New York: Twayne, 1953.

Tolson, Melvin B. *Caviar and Cabbage: Selected Columns by Melvin B. Tolson from the* Washington Tribune, *1937–1944.* Ed. Robert M. Farnsworth. Columbia: U of Missouri P, 1982.

———. *A Gallery of Harlem Portraits.* Ed. Richard M. Farnsworth. Columbia: U of Missouri P, 1979.

———. "The Odyssey of a Manuscript." *New Letters* 48 (Fall 1981): 5–17.

———. "A Poet's Odyssey" in *Anger and Beyond.* Ed. Herbert Hill. New York: Harper and Row, 1966. 181–195.

Walker, Margaret. "Review of *Rendezvous with America.*" Quoted in a collation of comments on *Rendezvous* among Tolson's Manuscripts, Library of Congress. Attributed to *New Adventures in Poetry.*

Werner, Craig Hansen. *Playing the Changes: From Afro-Modernism to the Jazz Impulse.* Urbana and Chicago: U of Illinois P, 1994.

Woodson, Jon. "Melvin Tolson and the Art of Being Difficult" in *Black American Poets Between Worlds, 1940–1960.* Ed. R. Baxter Miller. Knoxville: U of Tennessee P, 1988. 19–42.

The Harlem Group of Negro Writers

by

Melvin Beaunorus Tolson

Submitted in partial fulfillment of the requirements for the degree of Master of Arts in the Department of English and Comparative Literature, Faculty of Philosophy, Columbia University. June 1940.

Table of Contents

[Note: Table of Contents appears as in original thesis.]

FINIS

Preface

There are three aims in this thesis: first, to give the social background of the Harlem Renaissance and the various forces that scholars say operated in the black metropolis to bring about the artistic and literary development of "The New Negro"; second, to emphasize the lives and works of the leading contemporary Negro essayists, short story writers, novelists, and poets in the light of modern criticism; and, third, to interpret the attitudes and stylistic methods discovered in the Harlem Renaissance.

In order to achieve this three-fold purpose the writer interviewed several of the Harlem Group, securing literary and biographical materials, which in many instances had not reached the light of publication. In addition, the writer read all available books and articles covering twenty years of this period, and made extensive use of the Schomburg Collection; and, while the writer read the works of each author in the light of the author's aim, he has adhered to objective criticism rather than subjective evaluations; and where there were conflicting opinions these have been documented. The synthesized conclusions in this thesis represent, therefore, an initial attempt to collect the literary criticisms of this epoch in Negro life.

Without the invaluable suggestions of Dr. Rudolph Fisher, Mr. Wallace Thurman, Mr. Langston Hughes, Miss Zona Gale, Miss Harriet Monroe, Dr. Charles S. Johnson, and Dr. Arthur Christy, this thesis would be different in content and style.

Chapter 1

A Perspective of Harlem

Inscrutable His ways are, and immune
To catechism by a mind too strewn
With petty cares to slightly understand
What awful brain compels his awful hand.
Yet do I marvel at this curious thing:
To make a poet black, and bid him sing!

—Countee Cullen (from: "Yet Do I Marvel," *Color,* 1927)

And bards who from thy root shall spring
Will proudly turn their lyres to sing
Of Ethiopia's glory!

—Paul Laurence Dunbar (from: "Ode to Ethiopia," *Visions of the Dusk,* 1915)

Strange,
That in this nigger place
I should meet life face to face;
When, for years, I had been seeking
Life in places gentler-speaking,
Until I came to this vile street
And found Life stepping on my feet!

—Langston Hughes ("Aesthete in Harlem," *Opportunity,* 1930)

We are children of the sun,
Rising sun!

—Fenton Johnson (from: "Children of the Sun")

I hear America singing, the varied carols I hear . . .
Each singing his . . .
Always the free range and diversity!
Always the continent of democracy!

—Walt Whitman (first two lines from "I Hear America Singing"; last two lines from "Our Old Feuillage," *Leaves of Grass,* 1881–82)

The History of Harlem

The history of Harlem is a dramatic chapter in the narrative of the social development of America's metropolis. Peter Stuyvesant, in 1658, named the village New Haarlem after the old Haarlem in Holland from which the early inhabitants came. The Dutch village was founded "on the site of the camp from which the Indians had been turned out."[1] The village is described in Washington Irving's *Knickerbocker's History of New York.*[2]

However, the site of what is now Mount Morris Park was settled in 1636. A hundred years later a large number of immigrants from Germany, seeking opportunity and freedom in the new country, settled in that locality. Daily communication by horse railroad was established with New York in 1836. While it is true, as Paul Morand says, in his fascinating and elucidating book *New York,* that "the slaves brought from Brazil to New Amsterdam were not so prolific as they were in the South; many did not withstand the rigors of the climate, and others were burnt or hanged at the time of the great slave rising in the middle of the eighteenth century"[3]—the emi-

1. Paul Morand, *New York,* New York, Henry Holt, 1930, p. 265. [First published as *New York,* Paris: Flammarion, 1930. The English translation used by Tolson was that of Hamish Miles. For commentary of Morand's influence on Renaissance writers see Huggins, *The Harlem Renaissance,* pp. 90–91; 101 and 106.]
2. "Harlem," *Encyclopaedia Britannica,* Fourteenth edition, London, 1929, Vol. XVI, p. 200.
3. Paul Morand, *op. cit.*, p. 266.

nent Frenchman is wrong in maintaining that the flood of black migrants waited until the present century to inundate Harlem.[4]

The Recent Vogue of Harlem

Harlem is the unique product of New York City as the meeting-place of races and cultures in the Western Hemisphere.[5] Sociologists and fictionists have made intensive and extensive studies of this metropolis within a metropolis which have revealed, to eyes familiar only with ante-bellum and post-bellum Negro stereotypes, an El Dorado of racial dissimilarities, varying from the low-life characters of the rebel Jamaican's naturalistic *Home to Harlem*[6] to the dark intelligentsia of *Portraits in Color.*[7]

A serious student of Negro life makes the following observation concerning these diversities of the Harlem milieu:

> Harlem is unique in many respects. All types of Negroes mingle there. Every imaginable type of activity is carried on in this black city within a white metropolis.[8]

It is incontestable that ethnic groups obey the obligation and sanction of the law of voluntary and involuntary segregation. Harlem with its 276,421 people is no exception; but it must not be looked upon as "a quarter or a slum or a fringe."[9] Being a city in itself, Harlem has all the aspects of a diversified modern civilization, plus those differentiating customs, dialects, and modes of thought that Negro peoples have brought from all

---

4. Jerome Dowd, *The Negro in American Life,* New York, Century, 1926, p. 245.
5. Russell Blankenship, *American Literature,* New York, Henry Holt, 1931, p. 244.
6. Claude McKay, *Home to Harlem,* New York, Harper, 1928.
7. Mary White Ovington, *Portraits in Color,* New York, Viking Press, 1927. [The author Mary White Ovington (1865–1951) was a white socialist reformer who helped found the NAACP.]
8. Scott Nearing, *Black America,* New York, Viking Press, 1929, p. 122.
9. James Weldon Johnson, *Black Manhattan,* New York, Alfred A. Knopf, 1930, p. 3.

parts of the world. Alien ideas and native ideas, alien customs and native customs, sometimes remaining unchanged, but often coalescing and producing startling hybrids—these have colored the literature dealing with Harlem.

A City with Many Names

As a result of its many-sidedness, various names have been applied to Harlem in both current expression and in literature. Carl Van Vechten viewed Harlem as the Negro's terrestrial Elysium and called it "Nigger Heaven."[10] This Harlem of the cabarets caused the pleasure-seeking whites to storm the black city.[11] When one thinks of Harlem as the seat of the Garvey Back-to-Africa Movement, the National Association for the Advancement of Colored People, the Pan-African Movement, and other social or political organizations, then one sees its justification as "the capital of the Negro world."[12] Viewed from the angle of literature, Harlem has been vividly described as "the literary and artistic Mecca for Negroes."[13] Rudolph Fisher, the novelist and short story writer, undoubtedly epitomized the sentiments of the dark masses of his people when he made King Solomon Gillis call Harlem "The City of Refuge."[14] The name contains an imbedded analogy between events in Hebrew history and those in the ethnic experiences of the Negro migrants from the South.

---

10. Carl Van Vechten, *Nigger Heaven,* New York, Alfred A. Knopf, 1926, p. 15. [The full citation reads: "Dis place, where Ah met you—Harlem. Ah calls et, specherly tonight, Ah calls et Nigger Heaven! I jes' nacherly think dis heah is Nigger Heaven!" For a discussion of the reception of Van Vechten's novel see Jervis Anderson, *This Was Harlem,* 212–20.]
11. Rudolph Fisher, "The Caucasian Storms Harlem," *American Mercury,* Vol. II, pp. 393–398 (August 1927).
12. Arthur Warner, "The Negro's World Capital," *Dunbar News,* Vol. I, p. 5 (October 8, 1930). [Tolson was referring only to the title of the article in his quotation.]
13. Alain Locke, *The New Negro,* New York, Albert and Charles Boni, 1925, p. 7.
14. Rudolph Fisher, "The City of Refuge," *The Best Short Stories of 1925,* Ed. Edward J. Obrien. New York, Small and Maynard, 1925, pp. 105–121.

Terms in the Subject Defined

The area bounded by the Polo Grounds, the Harlem River, Morningside Avenue, Lexington Avenue, and 110th Street, is black Harlem proper.[15] Of course, on the outlying fringes of the black belt there is a white population that geographically comes within the compass of the term Harlem, but this thesis is not concerned with these. Moreover, one must not forget that the population of Harlem is continually pressing out, conquering new areas inhabited by those of other races and nationalities.

In this thesis the term Negro will be used in its sociological sense, the only way in which the concept bears any scientific significance. One of our foremost ethnologists has observed:

> We speak of Negroes in this country, but plainly this is nonsense if we are employing the word "Negro" in its biological sense. The American Negro is an amalgam, and the application of the term "Negro" is purely sociological.[16]

The Harlem group of Negro writers represents, then, those poets and novelists and short story writers of African descent who found expression in literature during the post-war period and who from the world's largest Negro city added a new body of poetry and fiction to "an expanding American literature."[17]

---

15. James Weldon Johnson, *Black Manhattan,* p. 146.
16. Melville J. Herskovits, *The American Negro,* New York, Alfred A. Knopf, 1928, p. 17. [Tolson's citation is to the last paragraph of the first chapter of "The American Negro: The Amalgam He Represents." The last sentence which Tolson elected not to quote reads as follows: "But the phrase 'American Negro' has real biological significance, and I shall attempt next to show that a physical type has developed from the mixture represented in his person."]
17. Harlan Hatcher, *Creating the American Novel,* New York, Farrar & Rinehart, 1935, pp. 140–151. [Tolson's citation is to the entire chapter "Exploiting the Negro." The exact quotation appears on p. 151.]

Chapter 2

The Negro or Harlem Renaissance

The Harlem Renaissance was a vast economic, social, religious, political, artistic, and literary movement which originated in the dark city about 1917, and which produced a psychologically different Negro known to sociologists, educationalists, and critics as the New Negro.[1] While the movement took on a national aspect, it served as a magnet to draw Negro talent to its center, Harlem.

It came with startling immediacy. A Negro poet and critic says: "Those who were in the midst of the movement were as much astonished as anyone else to see the transformation."[2] Obviously it was a phase of the post-war development in American literature. Professor Robert Kerlin reminds us that the Harlem Renaissance produced "a republic of letters within a republic of letters."[3] While both of these statements are true, a closer scrutiny reveals the

1. Alain Locke, *The New Negro,* New York, Albert and Charles Boni, 1925. [Tolson no doubt selected 1917 since James Weldon Johnson cites April 5, 1917, in *Black Manhattan* (p. 175) as the date three plays by black actors were performed at Madison Square Garden. For an excellent discussion of the early black theater see Jervis Anderson, *This Was Harlem,* 110–16.]
2. James Weldon Johnson, "Race Prejudices and the Artist," *Harpers,* Vol. 157, p. 771 (November 1928).
3. Robert Kerlin, *Negro Poets and Their Poems,* Washington, Associated Press, 1923, p. 1. [For a discussion of this book see Vilma R. Potter, "Race and

operation of definite forces, external and internal, that shaped and gave character to the movement. Dr. Alain Locke of Howard University in *The New Negro* has gone deeply into the underlying causes of the movement.

Factors in the Harlem Renaissance

Critics have compared the Harlem Renaissance with the literary movements in Dublin and Prague, and some of the articles in American magazines did a great deal to call attention to the works of Negro writers and familiarize the public with an interesting phase of American life.[4]

A study of minority groups shows that they are very sensitive to environmental forces and that this impressibility has a survival value. This characteristic is revealed in the factors that shaped the Harlem movement, and it has been pointed out by several prominent critics; in fact, so effective were these causes that Dr. Alain Locke summed up the case as follows:

> Within the past ten years more fiction has been published by Negro writers than had been put out by them in the preceding two hundred and fifty years. And every bit of this fiction—that is, every bit that has been published in a way calculated to reach the general public—has been written by the writers of the Harlem group.[5]

The limits of this essay will permit only a brief synthesis of these factors that produced the Harlem group.[6]

The World War and the Negro

The effect of the World War upon the Negro consciousness is not easily estimated. Wilson's "We must make the world safe for democracy" stirred

---

Poetry: Two Anthologies of the Twenties." Although Kerlin's anthology has a chapter, "The Present Renaissance of the Negro," Tolson's quotation is not found in this book.]

4. Carl Van Doren, "Negro Renaissance," *Century*, Vol. 111, pp. 635–637 (March 1926).
5. Alain Locke, *The New Negro*, p. 7.
6. John Chamberlain, "Negro as Writer," *Bookman*, Vol. 70, pp. 603–611 (Feb-

the imagination of all minority groups. A general spirit of restlessness swept over the country and the Negro was caught up in the wave of public sentiment. As a result, the young Negro with other Americans "sounded notes of revolt or resentment."[7] Negro writers broke away from the Dialect School of Dunbar and the ante-bellum and post-bellum stereotypes that had enslaved the literature of the race.[8]

The Cosmopolitanism of New York City

Literatures seem to thrive in the great catholic centers of the world. Francis Galton's remarkable study supports this generalization.[9] The cosmopolitanism of New York City has been conducive to the growth of culture from the earliest times down to the present day.[10] In such a liberal center, then, one finds the opportunities and the encouragement requisite for the cultivation of literary talent. And in the words of a novelist and critic who was one of the leaders in the movement: "New York has been almost exclusively the place where the emergence has taken place."[11]

White Patrons and Writers

White patrons and writers played a major role in securing an audience for many of the Harlem group, which was aided tremendously by the world interest in the dark city, its music, its art, its night-life. The mutual admi-

---

ruary 1930). [Tolson must have cited this for readers who wanted to read more on the topic since he does not use any of the information included.]

7. Ludwig Lewisohn, *The Creative Life,* New York, Boni and Liveright, 1924, p. 17.
8. V. F. Calverton, *Anthology of American Negro Literature,* New York, Modern Library, 1929, p. 13. [The citation should be to p. 11 where dialect is discussed.]
9. Francis Galton, *Hereditary Genius, An Inquiry into Its Laws and Consequences,* London, 1869.
10. Russell Blankenship, *American Literature,* p. 244.
11. James Weldon Johnson, *Black Manhattan,* p. 260.

ration of Henry L. Mencken and George Schuyler, the warm friendship of Carl Van Vechten and Langston Hughes, and the interest that Dorothy Scarborough, Edna Ferber, Clement Wood, Belasco, Carl Van Doren, and Eugene O'Neill manifested in Negro life had a healthful effect.[12] Dr. Charles S. Johnson of Fisk University has a very fine collection of letters relating to this phase of the movement.

One should not overlook the liberality of the great publishing companies like Albert and Charles Boni, the Viking Press, Alfred A. Knopf, Century, Harper's, and the Associated Publishers; nor magazines like *Century,* the *American Mercury,* the *Bookman,* and *Poetry;* nor newspapers like the *New York Times,* the *New York World,* the *Boston Transcript,* and the *Chicago Tribune*—organs of expression that made the Renaissance possible; that carried its achievements to a vast American public.

Fire *and* Harlem

The appearance of *Fire* and the publication of *Harlem,* two magazines sponsored by the younger members of the Harlem group, were events of maximal importance, though both were short-lived; and at another point in this essay, the records of these magazines will be discussed as they bear on the development of certain writers who were contributors to them or who served on the editorial staffs. *Fire* was the first Negro journal of artistic expression, for the other periodicals had been devoted to social and political problems.[13] The first issue appeared in November, 1926, and the board of editors consisted of Wallace Thurman, Gwendolyn Bennett, Richard Bruce, Zora Neale Hurston, Aaron Douglas, and John Davis.[14] Two years later Wallace Thurman put out the initial publication of *Harlem,* which set forth the stimulating aims of the younger group in a strident edi-

12. Elmer Carter, "Exceptional Whites," *Opportunity,* Vol. X, p. 85 (March 1932). [Belasco refers to David Belasco (1859–1931)]
13. "The Dark Tower," an editorial, *Opportunity,* Vol. V, p. 28 (January 1927).
14. "Board of Editors," *Fire,* Vol. I, p. 2 (November 1926). [*Fire* was reprinted in 1982 by The Fire Press, Metuchen, New Jersey. The reprint has two essays, "Lighting Fire" by Richard Bruce Nugent and "Fire in Retrospect" by Thomas H. Wieth, which appear on a printed insert.]

torial.[15] These magazines may be termed the voice of the Harlem Renaissance, and their pages contained the ambitious works of some who later achieved distinction.[16]

The National Association

The National Association for the Advancement of Colored People has been an asset in every activity for the development of the American Negro. Through its official organ, *The Crisis,* it has conducted literary contests and published the works of young poets and short story writers. It has had in its employ such well-known novelists as James Weldon Johnson, Dr. W.E.B. Du Bois, Walter White, and Jessie Fauset; and through them it has exercised a powerful influence.

Researches in Negro History

Students of Negro life have observed the changes in the attitude and tone of Negro literature since 1917. Mr. Arthur Schomburg would explain this by saying that when the Negro became aware of his past culture his inferiority complex began to disappear.[17] As president of the American Negro Academy and cofounder of the Negro Society for Historical Research, Mr. Schomburg has collected many items of historical interest and value to his race and the liberals of other races.

Another scholar who has contributed to this field is Dr. Carter G. Woodson, president of the Association for the Study of Negro Life and History and editor of *The Journal of Negro History.* Each year this organization conducts throughout the United States a Negro National History

15. Wallace Thurman, "High, Low, Past and Present," *Harlem,* Vol. I, p. 31 (November 1928).
16. "Editorial Board," *Harlem,* Vol. I, p. 4 (November, 1928).
17. Arthur Schomburg, "The Negro Digs Up His Past," *Anthology of American Negro Literature,* edited by V. F. Calverton, New York, Modern Library, 1929, p. 299.

Week, which receives enthusiastic support in churches and schools and newspapers.

Across this milieu of the dark metropolis moved those members of the Harlem group who gave expression to a racial life "through the medium of art, music or poetry."[18]

18. Paul Morand, *New York,* New York, Henry Holt, 1930, p. 275. [The same essay appeared in *The Survey Graphic* 6.6 (March 1925): 670–72.]

Chapter 3

Countee Cullen

His Life

Countee Cullen was born in New York City, May 30, 1903. He is the son of the Reverend R. A. Cullen, pastor and founder of Salem M.E. Church.[1] As a result, Cullen avers his "chief problem has been the reconciling of a Christian upbringing with a pagan inclination."[2]

He was educated in the New York public schools, and in 1922 he was graduated from the DeWitt Clinton High School. He was awarded while still in high school the first prize in a contest conducted by the Federation of Women's Clubs. His poem was suggested by Alan Seegar's "I Have a Rendezvous with Death."[3] Cullen called his poem "I Have a Rendezvous

1. Stanley J. Kunitz, "Countee Cullen," *Living Authors*, New York, H. W. Wilson, 1931, p. 89. [Tolson made frequent use of this source. The complete title is: *Living Authors. A Book of Biographies, edited by Dilly Tante [pseud.]*. New York: H. W. Wilson 1931. The most up-to-date bibliography is Margaret Perry's *A Bio-bibliography of Countee Cullen, 1903–1906*. For a study of his poetry see Houston Baker, *A Many-Colored Coat of Dreams: The Poetry of Countee Cullen.*]
2. Countee Cullen, *Caroling Dusk*, New York, Harper, 1927, p. 179.
3. Alan Seegar, "I Have a Rendezvous with Death," *Recent Poetry*, edited by Roy L. French, New York, D. C. Heath, 1926, pp. 177–178. [Tolson inadvertently referred to the poem as "A Rendezvous with Life" which has been corrected.]

with Life." Some years ago at a commencement exercise, Bishop Jones of the Methodist Episcopal Church affirmed that Cullen's poem was more philosophical and inspiring than Seegar's. Countee Cullen expresses his passionate attitude toward life in the following lyrical lines:

I have a rendezvous with Life
In days I hope will come
Ere youth has sped and strength of mind,
Ere voices sweet grow dumb;
I have a rendezvous with Life
When springs first heralds hum.
It may be I shall hear her soon,
Shall riot at her behest;
It may be I shall seek in vain
The peace of her downy breast;
Yet I would keep this rendezvous
And deem all hardships sweet,
If at the end of the long white way,
There Life and I shall meet.
Sure some will cry it better far
To crown their days with sleep,
Than face the wind, the road, and rain,
To heed the falling deep;
Tough wet, nor blow, nor space I fear,
Yet fear I deeply, too,
Lest Death shall greet and claim me ere
I keep Life's rendezvous.[4]

This poem reveals the depth and scope of the thinking of the young poet on the destiny that lay before him. From that moment he began to take writing seriously. Even at that time one could catch those sweet cadences and haunting rhythms that were to place him among the greatest lyricists of the twentieth century and cause an eminent critic to declare:

4. Countee Cullen, *Caroling Dusk,* p. 180.

> Wise white friends advise me that Cullen is not an authentic Negro poet. Possibly not. I find him to be what is more important: an authentic poet some of whose lyrics vie with the finest in America, regardless of color.[5]

In November of 1923 "To a Brown Boy"* appeared in *The Bookman.* In 1925 he received his A.B. and Phi Beta Kappa key from New York University. During the next year he took his A.M. from Harvard University. At that time he had established himself as a precocious student and a poet with a glowing future.[6] He has won several poetry contests, and in 1928 he traveled abroad on a Guggenheim fellowship in creative literature.

As a poet he is "a rank conservative, loving the measure line and skillful rhyme; but not blind to the virtues of those poets who will not be circumscribed . . ."[7] He resents patronage as a "Negro poet." He wants to be judged according to universal standards, and by them rise or fall.

For a while he was assistant editor of *Opportunity.* Later he made a successful tour that took him among the colleges and universities of New England. His lectures created a favorable reaction. At the present time he is teaching in the public school system of New York City.[8]

His principal published works are *Color, The Ballad of the Brown Girl, Copper Sun, The Black Christ and Other Poems, One Way to Heaven,* and *Caroling Dusk,* an anthology of Negro poetry, distinguished not only for its scholarly introduction and discriminating taste in the selection of the poems, but, also, for the fact that the biographical sketches were written by the poets themselves, save in the instance of Paul Dunbar, whose biographical data were given by Mrs. Alice Dunbar-Nelson, the childhood sweetheart and wife of the deceased. Dunbar was divorced by his wife, who later married a Delaware newspaperman.

At the beginning of his career Cullen was an admirer of Tennyson. Then he came under the influence of Edna St. Vincent Millay,[9] Housman,

---

5. Alfred Kreymborg, *Our Singing Strength,* New York, Coward-McCann, 1929, p. 576.

* [The poem with its homoerotic subtext was dedicated to Langston Hughes.]

6. "Harlem Life," *Survey,* Vol. 53, pp. 660–61. (March 1, 1925).
7. Countee Cullen, *op. cit.,* p. 180.
8. Stanley J. Kunitz, *op. cit.,* p. 89.
9. Elizabeth Lay Green, *The Negro in Contemporary Literature,* Chapel Hill, The University of North Carolina Press, 1928, p. 18. [Green notes only the

Robinson, and the immortal Keats. Keats is the poet whose quiet beauty has most affected the Negro singer. Read that poem of spiritual affinity penned by Cullen when spring was breathing new life through all nature:

> And you and I, shall we lie still,
> John Keats, while Beauty summons us?
> Somehow I feel your sensitive will
> Is pulsing up some tremulous
> Sap road of a maple tree, whose leaves
> Grow music as they grow, since your
> Wild voice is in them, a harp that grieves
> For life that opens death's dark door.
> Though dust, your fingers still can push
> The Vision splendid to a birth,
> Though now they work as grass in the hush
> Of the night on the broad sweet page of the earth.[10]

Concerning his philosophy as a poet facing the stress of modern life and moved by the spiritual realities within him, Cullen says:

> Most things I write, I do for the sheer love of the music in them. A number of times I have said I wanted to be a poet and known as such and not a Negro poet. Somehow or other, however, I find my poetry of itself treating of the Negro, of his joys and his sorrows— mostly of the latter— and of the heights and depths of emotion which I feel as a Negro.[11]

His Craftsmanship

There is little doubt that Countee Cullen has done a great service for American literature in renewing the interest of contemporary poets in the virtues

---

influence of Edna St. Vincent Millay. Tolson was most likely referring here also to James Weldon Johnson's observations in *The Book of American Negro Poetry*, pp. 219–220.]

10. Countee Cullen, "To John Keats, Poet at Springtime," *Caroling Dusk*, pp. 184–185.
11. Stanley J. Kunitz, *op. cit.*, p. 89.

of classic verse forms. The author of that excellent interpretation of recent poetry called *Our Singing Strength* pays this tribute to Cullen:

> He has not alone freshened up lyrical forms, but has mastered the witty and intellectual tests of old Greek and Latin epigrams.[12]

Professor Blankenship also observed this phase of Cullen's craftsmanship, and this discriminating critic in his discussion of "The New Poetry" expresses his views in the following manner:

> Countee Cullen is a born lyric poet with a gift for terse, epigrammatic expression. His poetry is a full-throated lyricism that is equaled only by the best singers in our literature. . . . Cullen's lines have a technical perfection seldom seen in contemporary verse. . . .
>
> But Cullen does not allow his great technical virtuosity, his lyrical gifts, or his talent for epigram to lead him away from his racial affiliations.[13]

In that narrative which tells the story of a young Negro, Jim, who was lynched for the sin of another man and who, Christ-like, dies and relives after death, Cullen wrought a work of moving intensity and graphic simplicity. The stamp of ethnic authenticity and a mature craftsmanship is upon it. His poem proves that he possesses "the quintessence of race-consciousness."[14]

Color[15]

Cullen's poems were now appearing in many of the leading magazines—all of them dipped in that brooding tragedy so diagnostic of his art: "Epitaphs,"[16] "Shroud of Color,"[17] "At the Wailing Wall of Jerusalem,"[18] and others.

---

12. Alfred Kreymborg, *op. cit.*, p. 580.
13. Russell Blankenship, *American Literature,* p. 645.
14. James Weldon Johnson, *The Book of American Negro Poetry,* New York, Harcourt, Brace and Company, 1922, p. 220.
15. Countee Cullen, *Color,* New York, Harper, 1925.
16. Countee Cullen, "Epitaphs," *Poetry,* Vol. XXVI, p. 204 (July 1925).
17. Countee Cullen, "Shroud of Color," *American Mercury,* Vol. III, pp. 306–08 (November 1924).
18. Countee Cullen, "At the Wailing Wall of Jerusalem," *Literary Digest,* Vol. 92, p. 34 (March 26, 1927).

Then came the book *Color* which caught the advertency of the critics with its richness of rhythms and imagery, blended into a pattern of inseparable parts which gave it an air of the impromptu discoverable only in the finest lyricists. It aroused in one critic memories of Edna St. Vincent Millay and A. E. Housman at their best.[19]

Babette Deutch, after discussing at length the character of Cullen's verse and the philosophy that wells up out of the intricacies of his craftsmanship, came to the conclusion that "the color of his mind is more important than the color of his skin."[20]

The singing quality of the lines was there, the effective handling of meter and rhyme, the pessimistic mood that did not lapse into pettiness. Irony was there, but nothing of the chilling fury of a Claude McKay or the cold bitterness of a Langston Hughes.

Copper Sun[21]

While critics observed that this book contained Cullen's usual rhythm, precise and unfailing, some thought that he did not give to poetry such individual rhythms as the Negro has contributed to music.[22] This was undoubtedly true, but when one recalls the fact that the minor rhythms of the Negro folk songs are the products of a racial heritage, containing strains that have come from a multitude of sources and were acted upon by a variety of social happenings, is it not an extraordinary thing to ask a poet to get those esthetic rhythms obtained by a whole people? Another critic contrasted *Copper Sun* with *Color:*

> *Copper Sun* is a very good book of verse, although not so good as the earlier *Color.* "From the Dark Tower," "Timid Lover," and "Variations,"

19. *Independent,* Vol. 115, p. 539 (November 1925).
20. Babette Deutch, "Countee Cullen," *Nation,* Vol. 121, p. 763 (December 1925).
21. Countee Cullen, *Copper Sun,* New York, Harper, 1927.
22. Elizabeth Lay Green, *op. cit.,* pp. 18–19. [These pages contain no reference to *Copper Sun.*]

> even though the last is a subject not more original than the loss of love, are only three of many very beautiful poems.[23]

Still another critic thought the volume contained "fifty-eight poems, charming, versatile, and satisfying."[24] Despite a dissenting note here and there, the prevailing opinion was that Cullen had not lost the magical touch of the earlier book. The poet's attitude toward the race problem in America is a subject that the student of the Harlem Renaissance continually encounters; but as Herbert Gorman says: "Best of all, he can forget that he is of the colored race and be just a 'poet' most of the time."[25]

Many distinctions have come to Countee Cullen in the field of literature, but perhaps his greatest was the receiving of the Harmon Gold Award for his contribution to creative poetry. He has written two of the most famous lines in the Western Hemisphere, and he is just beginning his artistic career. Professor James Weldon Johnson said concerning this tragic couplet:

> It is pardonable for me to repeat that the two most poignant lines in American Literature, lines that surged up from the vortex of these experiences, are in the sonnet of his in which he expresses faith that God can explain all the puzzling paradoxes of life; then, gathering up an infinity of irony, pathos, and tragedy in the final couplet, says:
>
> Yet do I marvel at this curious thing—
> To make a poet black and bid him sing.[26]

Perhaps the answer is obvious, after all: a poet must pass through the crucible of human sorrow. He must suffer in some dark Gethsemane in the world of experience, both physical and spiritual; then, and only then, can he sound the depths, the oceanic depths, of universal man.

Out of the sorrows of black and unknown bards—said Mr. Johnson himself—came the melancholy spirituals. Countee Cullen is black, with the

---

23. *Survey,* Vol. 59, p. 184 (November 1, 1927). [The critic is Gordon Lawrence.]
24. *World Tomorrow,* Vol. X, p. 472 (November 1927).
25. Herbert Gorman, "Countee Cullen," *Nation,* Vol. 125, p. 518 (November 9, 1927).
26. James Weldon Johnson, *The Book of American Negro Poetry,* p. 221.

tragedy of a race in his bosom; and for that very reason he should touch the world-heart with a deeper and darker beauty when he sings.

Did not the ancients think that the nightingale was nature's sweetest singer because it was a bird with a broken heart?

Chapter 4

Langston Hughes

I am Dark Youth
Seeking the Truth
Of a free life beneath our great sky.[1]

His Life

Countee Cullen and Langston Hughes represent the antipodes of the Harlem Renaissance. The former is a classicist and conservative; the latter, an experimentalist and radical. However, they are staunch friends and mutual admirers. With a biography that reads like a page from the *Arabian Nights,* Langston Hughes, the idealistic wanderer and defender of the proletariat, is the most glamorous figure in Negro literature.[2]

Langston Hughes comes from an old aristocratic family. He was born in Joplin, Missouri, on February 1, 1902. His father was a prominent lawyer and his mother a school teacher. His grandparents on his mother's

1. Langston Hughes, *The Negro Mother and Other Dramatic Recitations,* New York, Golden Stair Publishers, 1932, p. 19. [The poem is titled "Dark Youth of the U.S.A."]
2. Stanley J. Kunitz, "Langston Hughes," *Living Authors,* p. 184. [Tolson must be citing the biography as a whole since no similar analysis appears in Kunitz. For the most complete biography of Hughes see Arnold Rampersad's *The Life of Langston Hughes.*]

side belonged to that fortunate group known as Free Negroes before the Emancipation Proclamation was issued. They were a heroic pair, engaged in the dangerous activities of the Under Ground Railroad. The greater part of Langston's childhood was spent with his maternal grandmother, Mary Sampson Patterson Leary Langston, whose husband, Lewis Sheridan Leary, was one of the five Negroes with old John Brown at Harper's Ferry. The aged woman's husband was killed during the raid, and this maternal grandmother was later honored by President Theodore Roosevelt as the last surviving widow of John Brown's quixotic thrust at the slave system in the United States.[3]

During the Reconstruction Period there were two Negro senators and many black congressmen, and from Virginia came one by the name of John M. Langston, Hughes' granduncle. His grandmother married Charles Langston, a brother of this congressman, and they migrated to Kansas where the mother of the poet was born.[4]

Hughes spent his early boyhood in Lawrence, Kansas, the same town in which the grandmother of Wallace Thurman, the Harlem playwright and novelist, lived for many years before going to Salt Lake City. As a small boy, Langston visited Old Mexico where his father had "mountain property near the city of Toluca."[5] During his stay there an earthquake occurred. The awe-inspiring scene of thousands of kneeling figures crying and praying to a God who answered not still clings to his memory.

On the death of his grandmother, Langston went to live with his mother at Lincoln, Illinois. A few months later they moved to Cleveland, Ohio, where he attended the high school from which he was graduated in 1920. During this period he had written poems about factories, workers, and poverty, which were inspired by his reading of Max Eastman, Floyd

---

3. James Weldon Johnson, "Langston Hughes," *The Book of American Negro Poetry,* p. 232. [Johnson discusses the differences between Cullen and Hughes in his preface to Hughes's poetry. He in turn may have read the same idea in Elizabeth Lay Green's *The Negro in Contemporary American Literature,* "Two Younger Poets," pp. 18–21.
4. Countee Cullen, "Langston Hughes," *Caroling Dusk,* New York, Harper, 1927, p. 144.
5. Stanley J. Kunitz, *op. cit.,* p. 184. [See Edward J. Mullen, ed. *Langston Hughes in the Hispanic World and Haiti* for more on this connection.]

Dell, Claude McKay in the *Liberator,* and the poems of Carl Sandburg; these produced "the unconventionality of his work and style,"[6] which critics have observed.

This was followed by fifteen months spent with his father in Old Mexico. While there he learned Spanish, taught English in a business academy, and attended bullfights.[7] He also witnessed a revolution and saw three bandits hanged. He exercised his young body by furious riding through the open country and climbing the perilous sides of volcanoes. Here, too, he wrote "The Negro Sings of Rivers," his first poem to be published in a national magazine.[8]

In 1921 he came to New York City and entered Columbia University, which James Weldon Johnson had attended before him. Then came the break with his father, and he was compelled to earn his own living. For a while he worked on a Staten Island truck farm, and this was followed by his becoming a delivery boy for a New York florist.

But the wanderlust was in his blood, and for the next three years he entered a period of extensive travel. He became a member of a crew voyaging on a freight steamer to the Canary Islands and the Azores; then as a cabin boy he went to the West Coat of Africa, journeyed to the great Dakar Desert, drank palm wine with the natives of the Gold Coast, brought a monkey up the historic Niger, and almost ended his hectic career by falling into the Congo.[9] A few months later, feeling himself a real sailor, he returned to New York with his companionable monkey and six parrots.

In 1923 he made several voyages to Northern Europe and spent Christmas in Rotterdam, but February of 1924 found him stranded in Paris. He became doorman at a Monmartre night club on the Rue Fontaine, receiving for his work the tips and one meal a day. Since few Americans visited the place, the tips were conspicuously absent. The Grand Duc, where Florence Mills, the internationally famous black

---

6. Robert B. Eleazer, *Singers in the Dawn,* Atlanta, Education and Race Relations, 703 Standard Building, 1933, p. 17.
7. Countee Cullen, *op. cit.,* p. 144.
8. James Weldon Johnson, *op. cit.,* p. 234. [The poem was composed just outside of St. Louis en route to Mexico. See Rampersad, Vol. 1, 39.]
9. Stanley J. Kunitz, *op. cit.,* p. 184.

songster held forth nightly, needed a second cook.[10] Langston secured the job, but after he had seen the Olympic games he began, during the summer, his pilgrimage to Italy. The lure of the Italian lakes and the historic ruins held him in thrall until his money slipped away. Venice was the city of his misfortune. He tried to get back to Paris, where he would find American Negroes who might help him, but his passport was stolen in Milan.

Genoa is famous for its beachcombers: derelicts of all nations are to be discovered among them. Langston Hughes joined these outcasts, eating their figs and black bread. In his quest for beauty, unlike his friend Countee Cullen, Hughes found it among the flotsam and jetsam of life, whether he pilgrimaged in Europe or roamed a "nigger street" in Harlem.

Finally he secured a job as an ordinary seaman on a tramp steamer sailing for New York City; and for six weeks he painted bulk heads and scrubbed decks, while the schooner meandered in and out among the islands of the Mediterranean, thence past Sicily and Spain, before she crept through tossing seas back to the Statue of Liberty. From these experiences Hughes made many vivid and appealing poems, which are contained in *Fine Clothes to the Jew*[11] and *The Weary Blues.*[12]

The turning point in Langston Hughes' career came when he went to Washington, D.C., in 1924. First, he worked in the offices of Dr. Carter G. Woodson, the learned Negro historian and editor of the *Journal of Negro History.* Contact with this scholar from Harvard and the Sorbonne, who possessed a sublime faith in the future of the race in America, enriched the poet's ethnic experience.

But Langston Hughes never remains in one situation for any length of time. Later he became busboy at the Wardman Hotel in the capital. Mr. Lindsay, the poet who had done a fine piece of Negro characterization in "The Congo,"[13] was a guest at the Wardman. One evening Langston gave him three of his poems. Lindsay took them to his room with him and the

---

10. James Weldon Johnson, *op. cit.,* pp. 232–233.
11. Langston Hughes, *Fine Clothes to the Jew,* New York, Knopf, 1927.
12. Langston Hughes, *The Weary Blues,* New York, Knopf, 1926.
13. Roy L. French, "Vachel Lindsey," *Recent Poetry,* New York, Heath, 1926, p. 101.

very next day read them to an audience in the little theater of the hotel.[14] If one has heard Lindsay read and is aware of the fine dramatic materials of some of Hughes' poems, one can appreciate the wonderful impression that was made for the busboy poet by the itinerant minstrel from Springfield, Illinois.

From that moment of destiny, Langston Hughes became the object of public attention and Lindsay's words of encouragement set his goal before him. In 1925 he won the first prize for poetry in the *Opportunity* contest; and, in 1926, while a student at Lincoln University, Pennsylvania, he won the national Witter Bynner undergraduate prize in poetry for his poem "A House in Taos."[15]

The widespread interest in his poems is attested by the fact that many of them have been translated into German, Spanish, Russian, and Czechoslovakian, and some have been set to music. Hughes was also connected with the younger members of the Harlem group in the publication of *Fire* and *Harlem,* and his novel *Not Without Laughter* won the Harmon Gold Award in creative literature. In 1932 he went with a group of Negro actors to Russia to make a Negro picture under a Soviet director, and while there he wrote the poem "Goodbye Christ," which made the headlines in most of the Negro papers for three or four weeks. The controversy was very violent.[16]

In April of 1934 Langston Hughes published a short story in *Esquire;* the story was called "A Good Job Gone," and it caused the magazine to gain in circulation while at the same time it lost some subscribers and advertisers, because of the brutal realism with which Hughes described the tragic love affair of Mr. Lloyd, a white broker on Wall Street, and brown-complexioned Pauline, a Harlem dancer in the Cabin Club.[17] A variety of comments appeared in *Esquire's* "The Sound and the Fury," in regard to

---

14. Harriet Monroe, "Langston Hughes," *The New Poetry,* New York, Macmillan, 1932, p. 719. [See Rampersad, Vol. I, 117 for a discussion of the discovery.]
15. Stanley J. Kunitz, *op. cit.,* p. 185.
16. Melvin B. Tolson, "Goodbye Christ," *Pittsburgh Courier,* Vol. XXIII, pp. 10–11 (January 26, 1933). [See Robert Farnsworth, "What Can A Poet Do? Langston Hughes and Melvin B. Tolson."]
17. Langston Hughes, "A Good Job Gone." *Esquire,* Vol. 1, p. 46 (April 1934).

this Rabelaisian narrative told in the first person by a Negro student in dentistry, who was in attendance at Columbia.

Mr. Irwin S. Johnson wrote to the editors concerning the story as follows:

> You were rank traitors to your readers in leading them to expect something remarkable, something extraordinary. Your well-planned scheme of publicizing overshot its mark. "A Good Job Done" is perfectly harmless, even insipid.[18]

Mr. John Grimball Wilkins of Charleston, South Carolina, expressed his convictions with the holy passion of a zealot:

> This negro must have been born somewhere around the black belt of upper New York, or in the slums of Chicago in walking distance of the "Loop." He does not write like a genuine darky, he must have seen the south in the eyes of the regular off-shade "Yankee." Not one line of his story showed a clean thought, just gutter stuff.[19]

Mr. Joseph E. Idzal thought the controversy was much ado about nothing and that his suspicions concerning the pre-publication ballyhoo were justified when the story was published. Mr. Idzal thought the story was just another story, but he considered Langston Hughes a very good stylist.[20] On the other hand, Mr. Patrick Tyre at Tyler, Texas, was impressed with the plot and asked the editor to confess that the story had been written by Gertrude Stein.[21] Mr. R. A. Briggs was very much amused by the fury and he was glad that the editor published the story, for it was the direct cause of his beautiful friendship with a girl that he encountered on a Fifth Avenue bus.[22] Miss Doris Stead of New York said: "He knows people and beauty and feeling. . . . I hope you will print Mr. Hughes whenever he sends anything in."[23]

---

18. Irwin S. Johnson, "The Sound and the Fury," *Esquire,* Vol. 1, p. 15 (May 1934).
19. John Grimball Wilkins, *Ibid.*, p. 12.
20. Joseph E. Idzal, *Ibid.*, p. 12.
21. Patrick Tyre, *Ibid.*, p. 12.
22. R. A. Briggs, "The Sound and the Fury," *Esquire,* Vol. 1, p. 17 (May 1934).
23. Doris Stead, "The Sound and the Fury," *Esquire,* Vol. 1, p. 166 (June 1934).

In 1934 Hughes published a volume of short stories called the *Ways of White Folks.*[24] These stories had appeared previously in *Scribner's* and *Esquire.* The narratives were named "Cora Unashamed," "Slave on the Block," "The Folks at Home," "Passing," "A Good Job Gone," "Rejuvenation Through Joy," "The Blues I'm Playing," "Red-Headed Baby," "Poor Little Black Fellow," "Little Dog," "Beery," "Father and Son," "Mother and Child," and "One Christmas Eve." These stories depict the racial attitudes of whites and blacks when their lives touch each other.

Sherwood Anderson thought that Hughes possessed a fine talent, although the young Negro showed at times a seething indignation in some of the portrayals. Hughes, the rebel, is a bold enemy of economic and racial injustice and often his pen is dipped in the acid of satire. However, Sherwood Anderson observes further: "I do not see how anyone can blame him for his hatreds."[25] Hughes writes with a masculine vigor and each of the portraits is done with simplicity and integrity.

The poetic quality which obtains in Hughes' short stories is also revealed in his novel *Not Without Laughter,*[26] "which pictures the life of a poor family in Kansas and the cleavage between the hard-working, religious, conservative elder generation, and the young people coming to maturity in the jazz age, leaving the church and the submissions of the race for a freer life."[27] Harlan Hatcher, in his evaluation of contemporary fiction, does not hesitate to place the book "among the better novels."[28]

The Poetry of Hughes

Alfred Kreymborg says of Langston Hughes: "He is the poet laureate of Upper Seventh Avenue."[29] Of course, Mr. Kreymborg, not being a native of Harlem, got his streets confused. Seventh Avenue is the promenade of the

---

24. Langston Hughes, *Ways of White Folks,* New York, Knopf, 1934.
25. Sherwood Anderson, *Nation,* Vol. 139, p. 49 (July 11, 1934).
26. Langston Hughes, *Not Without Laughter,* New York, Knopf, 1930.
27. Harlan Hatcher, *Creating the Modern American Novel,* New York, Farrar & Rinehart, 1935, p. 151.
28. Harlan Hatcher, *Ibid.*, p. 151. [The quote reads: "Among the good novels."]
29. Alfred Kreymborg, *Our Singing Strength,* p. 577.

upper classes and the strivers.[30] However, we know what Mr. Kreymborg means. Langston Hughes is the chief ballad-singer of proletarian Upper Lenox Avenue, the street of "the unperfumed drifters and workers."[31] There is as evidence the prize poem "The Weary Blues," which pictures the Lenox Avenue locale, the poem that established Hughes as a poet.[32]

In this poem Hughes shows several of his notable attributes; he catches the undercurrent of philosophy that pulses through the soul of the Blues singer and brings the Blues rhythms into American versification. In this ethnic pattern he portrays in a few bold, impressionistic strokes the setting, the theme, the atmosphere, the pathos, the climactic suspense, the Negro character, and the odd denouement of the Blues; for the Blues, when racially authentic, have all the devices of an O. Henry short story with its surprising crack at the end.[33]

If an example of the original Blues-ballad is placed in juxtaposition with a Blues poem by the poet of Lenox Avenue, two things will be observed: the mastery of this racial form by Hughes and the accumulating repetition that brings the O. Henry surprise at the end. There is little doubt that this concentrated repetition reaches its highest degree of intensity in the Blues form, but it may be observed in other types of versification.

For example, Lafcadio Hearn traces it to the Norse in his discussion of repetition in the verse of Edgar Allan Poe, a lecture delivered at the University of Tokyo.[34] The "St. Louis Blues" is the most celebrated ballad of this type.[35] Of course the full effect of this ballad cannot be realized without the sad, sad rhythm of the melody. Here is an example from Hughes' "Po' Boy Blues."[36]

---

30. Rudolph Fisher, "Blades of Steel," *Readings from Negro Authors,* edited by Crowell, Turner, and Dykes, New York, Harcourt, Brace, and Company, 1931, p. 90.
31. *Ibid.*, p. 91.
32. Langston Hughes, *The Weary Blues,* New York, Knopf, 1926.
33. Dorothy Scarborough, *On the Trail of Negro Folk-Song,* Cambridge, Harvard Press, 1925.
34. Lafcadio Hearn, "Poe's Verse," *Interpretations of Literature,* New York, Dodd, Mead, 1926, pp. 150–166.
35. W. C. Handy, "St. Louis Blues," *Anthology of American Negro Literature,* p. 223.
36. Russell Blankenship, "Negro Poetry," *American Literature,* p. 642.

Weary, weary,
Weary early in de morn.
Weary, weary,
Early, early in de morn.
I's so weary
I wish I'd never been born.

If one has that sympathetic imagination which Mr. Mencken likes to talk about, one can, through identification of feeling, experience the utter physical and mental fatigue of that Negro after the cruel sleeplessness of the night-hours, facing the desolate flatness of another day. Langston Hughes understands the tragedy of the dark masses whose laughter is a dark laughter.[37]

Hughes has received much adverse criticism from the colored bourgeoisie, whom Dr. Melville J. Herskovits delights in calling "the most bourgeois of the bourgeoisie." They say his poems are "just like the nigger Blues," unmindful that this is the highest tribute they can pay to these artistic creations. Critics like Dorothy Scarborough and James Weldon Johnson consider the Blues as authentic a form of folk expression as the Spirituals are admitted to be, and Hughes has been able to catch the spontaneity and rhythm and philosophy of this ethnic expression. The Spirituals had a religious origin and the Blues a secular one.

No less an authority than Alfred Kreymborg asserts that there are instances in which Langston Hughes can give in a few lines "the implications of a full-length novel or play"[38] as he did in the poem "Cross":

My Old man's a white old man
And my old mother's black.
If ever I cursed my white old man
I take my curses back.

If ever I cursed my black old mother
And wished she were in hell,

---

37. Harlan Hatcher, "Sherwood Anderson," *Creating the Modern American Novel*, p. 169. [The reference is to Anderson's novel, *Dark Laughter*, 1925.]
38. Alfred Kreymborg, *Our Singing Strength*, p. 578.

I'm sorry for that evil wish
And now I wish her well.

My old man died in a fine big house,
My ma died in a shack.
I wonder where I'm gonna die,
Being neither white nor black.[39]

Has any other poet sung so poignantly about this tragic phase of American life? And to give point to Mr. Kreymborg's statement, Broadway has seen recently the dramatization of this theme in Langston Hughes' *Mulatto.* Professor Alain Locke, one of the best-informed scholars on the Harlem Renaissance, made this observation concerning the poet laureate of Upper Lenox Avenue:

> This work of Hughes in the folk-forms has started up an entire school of younger Negro poetry: principally in the *blues* form and in the folk-ballad vein. It is the latter that seems to be the most promising, in spite of the undeniable interest of the former in bringing into poetry some of the song and dance rhythms of the Negro.[40]

Professor Russell Blankenship sees in Hughes the jazz singer crooning in modern parlance the old, old woes of the black man,[41] while Mrs. Elizabeth Green, the wife of that talented interpreter of Negro life, Paul Green, discovers in Hughes "humor, abandon, and recklessness without self-consciousness."[42] Professor James Weldon Johnson admits that Hughes' work is motivated by race, but he hastens to add that "race means little to Hughes."[43]

39. Langston Hughes, "Cross," *The Book of American Negro Poetry,* edited by James Weldon Johnson, p. 236.
40. Alain Locke, "The Negro in American Culture," *Anthology of American Negro Literature,* edited by V. F. Calverton, New York, Modern Library, 1929, p. 256.
41. Russell Blankenship, *op. cit.,* p. 642. [Blankenship cites "Po'boy Blues" as an example of Hughes's careful use of dialect, p. 641.]
42. Elizabeth Lay Green, *op. cit.,* p. 20.
43. James Weldon Johnson, *op. cit.,* p. 234.

Now, the poet of Upper Lenox Avenue, who was not allowed to remain in Japan because of the red complexion of his economic philosophy and who was listed by the government of the United States as a dangerous political radical, would doubtless agree with Mr. Johnson on this matter.

Meanwhile, Charles A. Beard considers Langston Hughes one of the twenty-five most brilliant and social-minded personalities in America.[44]

44. *California News,* Los Angeles, Vol. X, p. 4 (June 21, 1935).

Chapter 5

Claude McKay

His Life

Claude McKay, the West Indian Negro whom no less a critic than Harlan Hatcher, in his elucidating volume *Creating the Modern Novel,* considers the best of the novelists coming out of Harlem and the "master of a crisp, poetic style," was born in Jamaica in 1889.[1] Writing from Poste Restante, Antibes, Alpes Maritimes, France, March 13, 1927, McKay, who made his reputation while still in Harlem, says: "My father was a peasant proprietor who owned his land and cultivated large tracts of coffee, cocoa, bananas, and sugar cane."[2] This knowledge of rural life is to be seen in his later works.[3] In fact, there is no member of the Harlem group who revels so inordinately in tropical luxuriance as Claude McKay.

His elder brother was a school teacher in the northwestern part of the island, and young McKay received his early education under this brother, "who was a free-thinker and the possessor of a good library in which there

1. Harlan Hatcher, *Creating the Modern American Novel,* New York, Farrar & Rinehart, 1934, p. 151. [For a good study of McKay see Tyrone Tillery, *Claude McKay: A Black Poet's Struggle for Identity.* Tolson himself published on McKay, see "Claude McKay's Art."]
2. Countee Cullen, *Caroling Dusk,* p. 82.
3. Elizabeth Lay Green, *The Negro in Contemporary American Literature,* p. 15.

were books by the great English scientists, novelists, and, above all, poets."[4]

By the time he was fourteen he had read all the writers, including Haeckel, Huxley, Arnold, and Shakespeare. The latter was his favorite, and many days were spent in the tropics with the mightiest of bards, days of dreaming during which McKay assimilated the culture which was to shape his future works.

At seventeen years of age he won a Jamaica Government Trade Scholarship, and despite his dislike of the work, he was apprenticed to a cabinet-maker and wheelwright. He soon left his job in disgust, and at nineteen he became a member of the Jamaica Constabulary.[5] At the end of ten months he left that position. With the assistance of a distinguished English scholar who was collecting Jamaican folklore, he was able to publish his first book, *Songs of Jamaica,* in 1911. These poems were written in the dialect of the island, and "they are veritable impressions of Negro life in Jamaica."[6]

The poems made McKay very popular in his native land and the young poet became known as the Burns of the West Indies. In 1912 he was given, in recognition of his ability, the medal of the Institute of Arts and Sciences, being the first Negro to receive that coveted honor.[7]

The following year he came to the United States, where he spent one year in Tuskegee Institute and two in the University of Kansas. Then he went to New York and at different times worked as porter, houseman, longshoreman, barman, railroad club and hotel waiter. During this period he was absorbing those exotic sounds, colors, dramatic incidents, comedies and tragedies that were to be painted into the foreground and background of his novels and poems.

Since that time Claude McKay has lived extensively abroad in Holland, Belgium, England, Russia, France, and Spain, but all his books, save the volume of poems called *Spring in New Hampshire,*[8] were published in the United States. Claude McKay first gained recognition as a poet; later as a

4. James Weldon Johnson, *The Book of American Negro Poetry,* p. 165.
5. Countee Cullen, *op. cit.,* p. 82.
6. James Weldon Johnson, *op. cit.,* p. 165.
7. Stanley J. Kunitz, *Living Authors,* p. 243.
8. Elizabeth Lay Green, *op. cit.,* p. 79. [Tolson is citing the *Book of American Negro Poetry,* p. 116.]

novelist and short-story writer. His third volume of poetry was named *Harlem Shadows*.[9]

Hodge Kirmon divided the poems of Claude McKay into three classes: first, the nature poems, such as "The Easter Flower," "Flame Heart," "The Tropics in New York," "Home Thoughts," "I Shall Return," and "The Subway Wind"; second, the poems of social significance, both racial and socioeconomic, as instanced in "America," "The Barrier," "In Bondage," "Lynching," "If We Must Die," "The Tired Worker," and "Dawn in New York"; and, third, the poems that express McKay's intense individuality, such as "Baptism," "French Leave," and "Spring in New Hampshire."[10]

Characteristics of McKay's Poetry

The reputation of Claude McKay as a poet will rest undoubtedly on his volume *Harlem Shadows*, although the other books contain here and there poems of real merit. At its best in this volume, McKay's work shows gradations of thought and feeling which he handles with surety of expression that makes him "not a great Negro poet—but a great poet";[11] and at times his poems contain the very essence of that which is beautiful and honest.[12]

We have observed that McKay came from a peasant ancestry and that his dialect verse showed his kinship with the life of the lowly. Moreover, in *Harlem Shadows* his rhythms caught the authenticity of his humble origins, and Mr. Rex Hunter discovered that the book possessed an "instinctive lyricism found in folk-songs."[13] But again and again McKay also sounds the spiritual revolt of the modern Negro. Perhaps the best summary of the elements in the style of this rebel Jamaican is to be found in the following criticism:

9. Claude McKay, *Harlem Shadows*, New York, Harcourt and Brace, 1922.
10. Hodge Kirnon, *The West Indian Review*, Vol. I, p. 17 (January–February 1932).
11. Walter F. White, ["The Negro Contribution,"] *Bookman*, Vol. 55, p. 531 (July 1922).
12. Rex Hunter, *Wisconsin Library Bulletin*, Vol. 18, p. 182 (June 1922).
13. Rex Hunter, *Ibid.*, p. 182.

> His work proves him to be a craftsman with keen perception of emotion, a lover of the colorful and dramatic, strongly sensuous, yet never sensual, and an adept in the handling of his phrases to give the subtle variations of the thoughts he seeks.[14]

Elizabeth Lay Green has observed in his poetry "a mystical merging of individual identify with that of race, pride in Africa's past, tenderness for all Negroes, bitterness for all who oppress them, and a defiance which mounts to flaming faith in the superiority of his people";[15] and yet this most violently revolutionary of Negro poets can forget his racial injustices and sing in sonnets "creating poetic beauty in the absolute."[16]

The Short Story Writer

In 1932 McKay turned his talent to the short story and produced *Gingertown,*[17] which included six narratives with Harlem as a background and six which had a Jamaican setting. McKay is a naturalist, and, while in his poetry he is often bitterly defiant in defense of his race, yet in his short stories and his novels he is unflinchingly realistic with the emphasis on the lower levels; and this has caused some racialists to say that it is surely no help to the Negro race to have them depicted as lewd, wanton, gross, vulgar, vicious, and incestuous. Thus, black respectables are scornful of Claude McKay.

He was very much at his best in that part of his book which dealt with the West Indian background in such stories as "The Agricultural Show," "Crazy Mary," "The Strange Burial of Sue"; and this quality of acrid poignancy is not matched in the narratives set against the background of Harlem. Rudolph Fisher, the Negro novelist and critic, observed in a private conversation "that strange West Indianisms issued from the mouths of

14. Walter F. White, ["Negro Poets,"] *Nation,* Vol. 114, p. 694 (June 1922).
15. Elizabeth Lay Green, *op. cit.,* p. 14.
16. James Weldon Johnson, *op. cit.,* p. 167.
17. Claude McKay, *Gingertown,* New York, Harper, 1932.

American blacks on occasion" when McKay seemed to get his Afro-Americans and Jamaicans confused.

The Novelist

Claude McKay's first novel, *Home to Harlem,*[18] deals with Jake Brown, who drifts from France to Harlem, after having lived a while in England. During his first night in Harlem he meets a little brown girl at the Baltimore Cabaret. He loses her, and the morning finds him alone with nothing but the memory of her companionship. Then follows a series of dramatic episodes in which Jake attempts to discover the whereabouts of his lost love. The plot of the novel is loosely constructed, but the Harlem pictures are unforgettable. Burton Rascoe declares:

> *Home to Harlem* is a book to invoke pity and terror, which is the very function of tragedy, and to that extent—that very great extent—it is beautiful. The language of *Home to Harlem,* whether Mr. McKay is setting forth in dialog a perfect transcription of Negro slang and dialect, or is telling his story in the Negro idiom, is a constant joy.[19]

The realism of *Home to Harlem* is stark and awful, but somehow it is beautiful. While McKay does not leave any detail unmentioned in the telling of the most sordid truths, these facts from the alleys of life lose their vulgarity because McKay relates them with the same simplicity that a child tells its mother this or that thing has happened. For that reason the book is an addition to our folklore, according to Professor Mark Van Doren.[20]

---

18. Claude McKay, *Home to Harlem,* New York, Harper, 1927. [For a good discussion of the impact of *Home to Harlem* see Jervis Anderson, *This was Harlem,* 220–23.]
19. Burton Rascoe, ["The Seamy Side,"] *Bookman,* Vol. 67, p. 183 (April 1928). [The last sentence of this quotation appears on p. 184. Tolson omits any sign like ellipses.]
20. Mark Van Doren, "Home to Harlem," *Nation,* Vol. 126, p. 351 (March 28, 1928).

Mr. Mortimer brings out a point which illuminates very clearly McKay's attitude toward his people, which has been criticized adversely on so many occasions that McKay has been compelled to defend himself and his art:

> Mr. Claude McKay writes of the less fortunate members of his race affectionately, but without illusion; he does not draw a moral, he is not superior.[21]

Banjo[22] was McKay's second novel. It uses the same episodic method which he had developed successfully in *Home to Harlem.* This book depicts the life on the swarming waterfront of Marseilles, where McKay was living at the time. One critic has said that *Banjo* "is less a story than a series of realistic pictures of the riffraff of the world thrown up in the slum areas along the docks."[23] *Banjo* contains the stylistic devices of the first novel, the chief difference being the dissimilarity of the locale.

In *Banana Bottom* published in 1933, Claude McKay returned to the rich, exotic life of his native Jamaica.[24] The heroine, Bita Plant, is a native brown girl of the Banana Bottom Settlement. Soon Bita is adopted by some white missionaries and sent to England to be educated. Years later she returns, a cultivated and refined woman. Then begins her struggle with the unkindly forces of her environment; and the story ends with her acceptance of the inevitable in her marriage to an uneducated native farmer.

This book contains the poetic beauty of the other, for McKay is a poet at heart: one is made to feel the glamour of the tropics and twilight beauty of palms, ferns and hibiscus, also the fury of the hurricane; but here McKay goes beneath the provincial scene, revealing the questions which the writer had observed in many lands and among many peoples.[25] McKay is like his favorite character Ray in *Banjo,*[26] forever probing at the eternal *why* of existence.

---

21. R. Mortimer, "Claude McKay," *Nation and Athenaeum,* Vol. 43, p. 397 (June 23, 1928).
22. Claude McKay, *Banjo,* New York, Harper, 1929.
23. Stanley J. Kunitz, *Living Authors,* p. 243.
24. Harlan Hatcher, *Creating the Modern American Novel,* p. 151.
25. *Nation,* Vol. 136, p. 564 (May 17, 1933).
26. Claude McKay, *Banjo,* p. 313.

Claude McKay, perhaps the first Negro intellectual apostle of Marx, is terribly perturbed by what he sees in civilization, especially the contradictions and brutalities.*

Skillfully he portrays the conflicting attitudes of races, white and black and Asiatic, in the islands; but he does not cater to his love for sensational drama, because he wants you to know, feel, and understand these groping characters, and thus the novel takes on many of the attributes of the folk tale.[27] The book is like a black and white sketch with its contrasts of humor and pathos, and it possesses "the quiet charm of introspective analysis."[28]

Claude McKay saw the dynamic possibilities in Negro life. As one of the early members of the Harlem Renaissance, he has sought to depict the many-sidedness of his people. At least one critic does not hesitate to place him in the category of the greatest living writers of the world.[29]

---

* See Geta LeSeur, "Claude McKay's Marxism."

27. *Nation,* Vol. 136, p. 564 (May 17, 1933).
28. *Saturday Review of Literature,* Vol. 9, p. 529.
29. Stanley J. Kunitz, *Living Authors,* p. 243.

Chapter 6

Walter White

His Life

Walter White, novelist and essayist, has made his home in Harlem since his graduation from Atlanta University, located in the capital city of Georgia, where he was born. James Weldon Johnson also attended this institution, and for a long while Dr. W.E.B. Du Bois served there as the professor of sociology. After an absence of many years, Dr. Du Bois returned to his old position.

By a strange coincidence these three men later encountered each other in New York City and worked together on the staff of the National Association for the Advancement of Colored People.

Since 1918 Walter White has been Assistant Executive Secretary of the National Association and "has done significant work in investigating lynchings and race riots,[1] because he is so light-complexioned that he is able to pass for a Caucasian. He has contributed to many periodicals and is the author of two novels and a fine history, which is an authoritative study of the lynching evil in the United States.[2]

---

1. V. F. Calverton, *Anthology of American Negro Literature,* p. 535. [Little has been written on White. See Charles F. Cooney, "Walter White and the Harlem Renaissance" as well as David Levering Lewis, *When Harlem Was in Vogue,* 130–43, 248–49, 267.]
2. Elizabeth Lay Green, *op. cit.,* p. 441. [The citation is to Calverton, p. 535.]

From time to time he has given the world the dramatic personal stories of his harrowing experiences as an investigator;[3] the series that ran in the *New York World,* depicting a lynching in South Carolina, aroused the indignation of the civilized portions of the globe. Walter White has been able to mix with the mobs and get the facts in each case that he investigated personally.[4]

Very little is known about the private life of Walter White; yet perhaps the name of no other Negro appears so often in the public press. He is a sort of stage character. His startling disappearances and dramatic entrances have caught the attention of vast numbers of people and held their interest. It is this octoroon who is the only Negro in public life who has received no adverse criticism on the role that he has played, often at the risk of his life.

Fire in the Flint[5]

Walter White's first novel was the story of Dr. Kenneth Harper, a Negro physician who graduated from Harvard Medical College and returned to Georgia to practice his profession, only to have his sister raped by poor whites and his brother burned through a mad attempt to avenge the dishonor of his sister, and finally to suffer death at the hands of the mob. Walter White is always the journalist setting down in staccato style the things he has seen and heard. He does not possess the mastery of craftsmanship which one finds in Rudolph Fisher or Claude McKay, but he tells his story in a straight-forward manner.

Fire in the Flint created a great amount of comment on account of its theme. It was debated pro and con. On the campus of the University of Georgia students read it with avidity. The Negro press and the Negro colleges found in the narrative materials for animated discussions.

---

3. Elizabeth Lay Green, pp. 112–115. [The citation is to p. 44 where Green discusses both *The Fire in Flint* and *Flight.*]
4. Mary White Ovington, *Portraits in Color,* New York, The Viking Press, 1927, p. 110.
5. Walter White, *Fire in the Flint,* New York, Knopf, 1924. [See George Hutchinson, *The Harlem Renaissance,* pp. 348–49 and 382–86 for the publication history of the novel.]

Although many critics discovered in the book defects in artistic portrayal, the authenticity of the work as an accurate chronicle of Southern life was not doubted. One reviewer in a prominent literary magazine said:

> It is told with a sort of passionate vigor that sweeps you over the faults in characterization to a finish which, to me, is inevitable and therefore not melodramatic.[6]

Mr. Panghorn discussed it in an interesting article. He was impressed by its colossal upward accentuation, the way in which the incidents gradually and steadily gathered themselves in a final cumulative effect for the inevitable tragedy.[7]

On the other hand, Konrad Bercovici, the novelist and short story writer, examined the book in the perspective of the historical background of the American novel and concluded: "The result is a stirring novel, beautifully and passionately written, the exact like of which has never been seen in the United States."[8]

The fingerprints of the novice are seen in the pages of the narrative; it bears the stamp of the news story trying to beat the deadline. However, it contains objective truth; it lives and breathes with a terrible reality. It is the intense story of a man who has seen humanity naked in the marketplace and has hastened to tell his fellows.[9]

Flight[10]

Walter White, like Jessie Fauset, the leading woman novelist of her race, went to the octoroon for his second novel, and the result was *Flight,* the

---

6. *Bookman,* Vol. 60, p. 342 (November 1924). [The quotation appears in an article entitled "The Book Editor Recommends" by J. F.]
7. H. L. Panghorn, "Fire in the Flint," *Independent,* Vol. 115, p. 850 (November 1924).
8. Konrad Bercovici, ["Almost White and Black,"] *Nation,* Vol. 119, p. 388 (October 8, 1924).
9. Harlan Hatcher, *Creating the Modern American Novel,* p. 148. [Hatcher only refers to *Fire in the Flint* on p. 147.]
10. Walter White, *Flight,* New York, Knopf, 1926.

tragic story of the Creole Mimi, a narrative which begins in New Orleans, moves through Atlanta, Philadelphia, Harlem, and Paris, and finally ends with the return of Mimi to her people, after having married and left a white man whom she did not love and understand.

Walter White has "passed" so often that he could easily put himself in the place of Mimi and give an uncommonly good picture of her emotional reactions to the new world that she entered.

Dean William Pickens of Morgan College, but more recently connected with the N.A.A.C.P., said in a lecture at Lincoln University in 1919 that 50,000 octoroons had faded into the white race, and that, on account of the greater opportunities, hundreds were following their examples every year. Negroes discuss among themselves, friends and relatives, many in high circles socially and financially, who have become "white." Most of them pass for good, many temporarily, and others move back and forth across the color line for the sake of adventure, or to discover facts from the socially superior group that would be of advantage to their own people.

Flight is an excellent document of modern American life in the crucible of race relationships, but "as a novel, it is heavy-footed."[11] It is lacking in artistic distinction, despite its being, in the words of Mr. J. W. Crawford, "a disturbingly serious book."[12] The propagandist in Walter White overshadows the novelist, and his chief contribution to fiction is of a social nature, a documenting of cases that he has discovered in his forty investigations of Judge Lynch.[13] His style is typically journalistic, and it was acquired under the pressure of editorial urgencies— the only way that one can become a competent journalist, according to Dr. Robert M. Hutchins of the University of Chicago.[14]

Ideas and realities interest Walter White more than craftsmanship, and in the passionate rush and upsurge of presenting them, like Upton Sinclair, he tramples art for art's sake under foot.

---

11. *Independent,* Vol. 116, p. 555 (November 8, 1926).
12. J. W. Crawford, "Flight," *Independent,* Vol. 116 (June 1, 1926).
13. *Saturday Review of Literature,* Vol. 2, p. 918 (June 10, 1926).
14. "Hutchins on Journalism Schools," Editorial, Vol. XVII, No. 42, p. 4 (February 26, 1938).

The Investigator

Rope and Faggot was White's third book, a purely scientific study of Judge Lynch. It was a work for which he was admirably prepared. The critics were loud in their praise of the book. White has profited by the variety of his interracial contacts; as his friend and co-worker, Mary White Ovington, has observed: "His Harlem apartment is a meeting place for distinguished men and women who love their glimpse into a new social world."[15] His approach, then, is many-sided in its catholicity and objectivity.

Thus he was fitted to study some 4,000 cases of lynchings in the United States and to analyze the causes. His investigations revealed three principal motivating influences: the economic, the sexual, and the religious. He found that few of the blacks who were lynched had ever been accused of rape, but that economic competition, religious fanaticism, and the sexual jealousy of the lower elements of the white population had actuated most of the mobs; and that the better classes of whites and the communities with the highest levels of intelligence and culture participated in comparatively few lynchings.[16]

Walter White was dealing with savage and gruesome happenings, all the more atrocious since he had seen more cases of lynchings than any other living man in America; yet Mr. Irving Astrachan believed that in the "presentation of facts, Mr. White maintained an admirable detachment."[17] On the other hand, Mr. Ellsworth Faris was very much interested in the social effect of the volume and predicted that it would do a great amount of good in removing the stigma of the rapist from vast numbers of the American population.[18]

Walter White is the only one of the four Harlem novelists that worked together on the staff of the *Crisis* now left to carry on the research and propaganda of the National Association for the Advancement of Colored People. Dr. W.E.B. Du Bois is the professor of sociology at the new Atlanta

---

15. Mary White Ovington, *Portraits in Color,* p. 116.
16. Walter White, *Rope and Faggot,* New York, Knopf, 1929.
17. Irving Astrachan, "Rope and Faggot by Walter White," *Bookman,* Vol. 69, p. 447 (June 1929).
18. Ellsworth Faris, ["The Cave Man Within Us,"] *New Republic,* Vol. 58, p. 338 (May 1929). [Tolson expands on Farris's brief comments.]

University; Dr. James Weldon Johnson is the professor of creative literature at Fisk University; and Jessie Fauset is teaching French in a New York high school.

It is said that when a detective becomes well known he is no longer a good detective for he is a marked man. This maxim seems to apply to Walter White as an investigator of lynchings. The N.A.A.C.P. has forced him to give up his dangerous field work, and now he is initiating plans for the organization from the offices of the *Crisis*. He has been summoned time after time before the Congressional Committee on Lynching, and he has probably done more than any other man to build up a sentiment against this heinous practice which he has reported so graphically in *Fire in the Flint*, *Flight*, and *Rope and Faggot*.

Chapter 7

Eric Walrond

His Life

Eric Walrond, the short story writer, was born in British Guiana in 1898, traveled extensively in other countries, and finally settled in France, after having spent many years in Harlem, as one of the younger members of the Negro Renaissance. His education was marked by an interesting variety, being acquired in Colon, at the College of the City of New York, the University of Wisconsin, and Columbia University. Zona Gale was very much interested in his artistic talent and helped secure for him a fellowship at the university in her native state. For many years, she has been a patron and friend of exceptional Negroes, among them Jessie Fauset the novelist; Booker T. Washington the educator; Colonel Young the soldier-bibliophile; and Dr. Charles S. Johnson the only Negro member of the Rosenwald Foundation.[1]

Eric Walrond's resident in Panama, where he served some time as a journalist, gave him the rare opportunity of absorbing the exotic color of the tropics and of studying the many-hued races that move through the

1. Footnote: Data secured from Miss Zona Gale (Mrs. William L. Breese) at Portage, Wisconsin, during an interview. [According to Robert Farnsworth, the interview took place on Thanksgiving Day, 1932. See *Plain Talk,* p. 40. For a discussion of the role played by Gale in the Renaissance see George Hutchinson, *The Harlem Renaissance in Black and White,* 214–16.]

day-life and night-life of the Canal Zone.[2] For a while he was on the staff of *Opportunity,* one of the two leading magazines of the Negro scene, and he has contributed to *Current History, The American Caravan,* the *New Republic,* and other periodicals. He is a literary critic of nice discrimination, whose well-timed articles aided considerably in spreading the seeds of the Harlem Renaissance.

As a short story writer Eric Walrond has gained a respectable niche among contemporary craftsmen in the art. He has proved "that the Negro may be judged as an artist with no special consideration because of race."[3] The publication of *Tropic Death,*[4] a group of short narratives, centered the attention of critics on this stylist whose reproductions of sense impressions of heat, thirst, terror, and desire in the tropics and of their effects on peasant and derelict, together with the "readily understandable transcriptions of different dialects,"[5] revealed a vivid authenticity.

Half-tamed jungles, color-struck seas, scrawny peasant villages, and teaming white, yellow, brown and black workers moving in and out of English, Spanish and French cities form the bizarre setting for Mr. Walrond's graphic and sometimes incomplete bits of action.

Elements of His Craftsmanship

There are critics who maintain that the short story is the most exacting type of prose composition. More short stories are written than any other literary type; yet fewer masterpieces are given to the world. Moreover, there seems to be greater scope for differences of opinions among the critics themselves.[6] Our flood of anthologies is conclusive proof of this.

---

2. Footnote: Information secured from Mr. Walrond during an interview after his trip to France.
3. Elizabeth Lay Green, *The Negro in Contemporary American Literature,* p. 51.
4. Eric Walrond, *Tropic Death,* New York, Boni and Liveright, 1926. [See Carl A. Wade, "African-American Aesthetics and the Short Fiction of Eric Walrond: *Tropic Death* and the Harlem Renaissance."]
5. Elizabeth Lay Green, *op. cit.,* p. 53.
6. Blanche Colton Williams, "Introduction," *Prize Stories of 1922,* edited by O. Henry Memorial Award Committee, New York, Doubleday & Page, 1922, p. 9.

The contrast between Eric Walrond's method and that of Julia Peterkin is quite illuminating. Mr. Walrond's point of view is almost entirely that of a spectator describing his impressions with utter detachment and objectivity, while Mrs. Peterkin passes "most of her impressions through the minds of her characters."[7] So well does she do this that it is related that a student asked his English teacher if Mrs. Peterkin were a Gullah Negro. The way Mr. Walrond ranged over the islands of Jamaica, depicted the teeming multitudes that helped to build the Panama Canal, dipped into Honduras and the jungles of the Guianas of South America—this stylistic device employed with telling artistry led Paul Rosenfeld to compare Walrond with Jean Toomer and Waldo Frank and to say that "Again a creative power has arrived for American literature."[8]

However, Mr. V. F. Calverton voiced a complaint that came like a discordant note in a symphony:

> [The stories] are diffuse in narration, tardy in climax, and often tedious in conclusion. Despite the freshness of the prose, its movement is delayed by detail that is superfluous and encumbered by filigree that is futile.[9]

But is not there a unique harmony of the movement in the narration with the phlegmatic activity of life in the tropics? Is not the rush and stress of the American scene well matched in the prose of Ernest Hemingway by the sharp, incisive pace of his narrative style? Eric Walrond, having lived in the tropics, knew the sluggish nature of all living things in the devitalizing heat of that region, the gradual disintegration, the physical and cerebral languor; and he had the artistic competence that enabled him to adapt his prose to the primitive, leisurely rhythms of the equatorial reality.

---

7. Elizabeth Lay Green, *op. cit.*, p. 51. [For a discussion of Peterkin's role in the Renaissance, see George Hutchinson, *The Harlem Renaissance*, 201–02 and 245–46.]
8. Paul Rosenfeld, *Men Seen*, New York, Dial Press, 1925, p. 232. [The correct quotation reads: "Again a creative force has arrived for American literature." There is no mention of Walrond by Rosenfeld.]
9. V. F. Calverton, ["Ground Swells in Fiction,"] *Survey*, Vol. 57 (November 1, 1926), p. 160.

Mr. Robert Herrick brings forward three points of major consideration in his discussion of these stories, so singularly different from any other in our category of the short narrative:

> The ten short stories gathered in *Tropic Death* have three separate sources of distinction which differentiate them from contemporary fiction. They are almost the virgin working of a rich new field, the black West Indies, where the seething mass of conglomerate races and colors provide the mobile labor force needed to exploit the tropics . . . Walrond handles this material from the inside, as a Negro with, one suspects, direct experience of the labor gangs. This is the second distinction. The third is a personal triumph. Walrond is an artist working not imitatively in subservience to the accepted literary traditions of an alien race, but his own manner suited to his own material— as an equal.[10]

It is true that Eric Walrond is an independent artist and that his images are not blurred by either sentiment or prejudice, nor is there freshness dimmed by the commerce of alien hands. At present he is living in an old chateau near Paris, "where he can secure a better perspective for the portrayal of Negro character in the Americas."[11]

---

10. Robert Herrick, "Tropic Death," *New Republic,* Vol. 48, p. 332 (November 10, 1926).
11. Footnote: Quoted from a letter written by Mr. Walrond, which is in the possession of the writer.

Chapter 8

Rudolph Fisher

His Life

Rudolph Fisher, physician, critic, short story writer, and novelist, was born in Washington, D.C., on May 9, 1897.[1]

His father was a Baptist preacher who was born during the days of slavery, and, like many another Negro, when the Civil War came, he was drafted into the Confederate army and by military law forced into the job of muleteer. He had always yearned for freedom; so, when the opportunity came, he ran away, hotly pursued by a squad of rebels. He arrived at the bank of a river. All hope had expired in his heart, when suddenly he descried a pontoon bridge, and over this he fled to safety in a Northern army camp.

For any years he worked as a blacksmith in and around New Orleans, and then he made his way up to Little Rock, at that time a town with many features of the frontier. By the time he was thirty he had taught himself to read the Bible, and then his vocation became farming and his avocation

1. Footnote: Biographical data secured from Mr. Fisher himself during an interview for this thesis. Mr. Fisher died on December 26, 1935. These facts have not appeared elsewhere. [For an overview of Fisher's role in the Renaissance see George Hutchinson, *The Harlem Renaissance in Black and White,* 403–4; David Levering Lewis, *When Harlem was in Vogue,* 229–30; and Nathan Huggins, *Harlem Renaissance,* 118–21.]

preaching. Through industry and shrewdness he accumulated large holdings in agriculture, which incited the jealousy of his white neighbors.

One dark night his house was attacked by night-riders, and he repulsed them with gunfire. The countryside was aroused. White farmers took down their muskets, and indignation spread like a livid flame among those who had defended the Lost Cause. The blacks of the region stayed indoors. Mr. Fisher and his family, after many hazards, reached New York. Perhaps that is the reason the dark metropolis has always been to Rudolph Fisher "a City of Refuge," the title of his most famous short story.

Some months later the mother of the novelist was with child, so she gained the reluctant consent of her husband to return to Little Rock, where her people lived, in order to be under their immediate care. Harlem was a strange place to her, a terrifying place.

En route, she stopped in Washington, and during the interval between trains the future novelist was born. When the eminent physician tells about this phase of his life, he chuckles and says that he hastened his arrival so that he might not be born "on the unholy soil of the holy South." He has never crossed the Mason and Dixon Line.

Later the family went to Providence, Rhode Island, where young Rudolph attended the public schools. His father wanted him to have the best education possible. Education was an obsessing principle with the old man. He hated the South because it had kept him from realizing his intellectual ambitions. Having finished high school in Providence, Rudolph entered Brown University, from which he secured the degrees Bachelor of Arts and Master of Arts.

He won a scholarship each year on the basis of the grades that he made in his classes. He also took the prize in German, and for this he was publicly commended by President W. H. P. Faunce.[2] During his junior year he represented Brown University in the intercollegiate oratorical contests held at Harvard, in which the contestants came from Harvard, Yale, Dartmouth, and Amherst. His subject was the popular one at the time, "Prohibition." He argued in its defense and won the first prize. He was class ora-

2. Footnote: Materials secured from Mr. Fisher's *SCRAPBOOK,* which he was kind enough to let me study for this thesis. Since Mr. Fisher's death, I do not know what became of this material.

tor, commencement speaker, and besides took honors in both biology and English.

Rudolph Fisher is one of the few men in America who have won the Delta Sigma Rho key in public speaking, the Phi Beta Kappa in scholarship, and Sigma Xi in science. He became an assistant in biology at Brown, but later entered Howard University in Washington, D.C., to study medicine. At Freedman's Hospital he became an x-ray technician; and in 1925 his last year at Howard University, he wrote that now famous story "The City of Refuge."

His stories and criticisms have appeared in many magazines, and his favorite narrative is "Fire by Night." Fisher is not concerned with the race question in these stories, and he usually follows the method that Edgar Allan Poe used— that is, Fisher writes his last paragraph first.[3] He won the Amy Spingarn Prize in the short story— a story in which, as usual, one discovers the harmony of plot, character, and atmosphere.[4]

Mr. Fisher told the writer that one day Blanche Knopf asked him to write a novel, and his friend E. O. Austin bet him that he could not write a novel in which the high life and low life of Harlem would be integrated. The result was *The Walls of Jericho.*[5]

Mr. Fisher's favorite writers are Wells, Shaw, Conrad, Bennett, Dorothy Parker, Thomas Beer, and Rebecca West. He thinks that *If Winter Comes* is a novel that will go down to posterity, despite what critics may say to the contrary.

His Short Stories

Rudolph Fisher has carved a unique place for himself as a writer of short stories. No member of the Harlem group is more adept in this sphere of artistry. He is exceptionally clever at plot-making; and some of his stories, like "Blades of Steel,"[6] bring to mind the famous O. Henry twist. The best

---

3. Footnote: This comment on Mr. Fisher's technique was received during the interview.
4. Elizabeth Lay Green, *op. cit.,* p. 54.
5. Rudolph Fisher, *The Walls of Jericho,* New York, Knopf, 1928.
6. *Readings from Negro Authors,* edited by Cromwell, Turner, and Dykes, New York, Harcourt, Brace and Company.

of the short narratives are "The City of Refuge,"[7] "Ring Tail," "The Promised Land," "High Yellow," "The Shadow of White," "Harlem Sketches," "The Back-slider," and "Fire by Night." Frazier Hunt bought two of the stories for *Cosmopolitan,* which boasts of its big names; at that time Fisher was little known, and so Ray Long, the editor-in-chief, switched the stores to *McClure's.*

A Novel of Ratiocination

Mr. Fisher was the first Negro to write a novel of ratiocination. It bore the title *The Conjure-Man Dies,*[8] a puzzling mystery which enabled Fisher to bring in some of his esoteric knowledge of the medical science and at the same time to paint a lively picture of Harlem and its multiple types of Negroes.

Mr. W. C. Weber observed its adroitness, humor and clever plot and considered it "among the best of the current output."[9] Fisher delved deeply into the primitive superstitions that illiterate migrants from the bayous of Louisiana and the Big Delta of Mississippi had brought into Harlem during the World War Period—native superstitions bearing the vestiges of their African origins. Carl Van Vechten had caught snatches of the voodoo scenes in the Black Mass with its demoniac saxophones wailing, its tom-tom beating, and its nude woman dancing on an illuminated floor of glass.[10] But newness and originality marked this first long story of ratiocination with Negro characters by a Negro.

7. *Best Short Stories of 1925,* edited by Edward O'Brien, New York, Small & Maynard, 1925. [See Eleanor Q. Tignor, "The Short Fiction of Rudolph Fisher."]
8. Rudolph Fisher, *The Conjure-Man Dies,* New York, Covici, 1932.
9. W. C. Weber, "The Walls of Jericho," *Saturday Review of Literature,* Vol. 9, p. 47 (August 13, 1932).
10. Carl Van Vechten, *Nigger Heaven,* New York, Knopf, 1926, pp. 255–260. [The reference is to chapter six. The scene alluded to appears on pp. 254–56.]

A Novel of Distinction

Critics seem to agree on three things concerning Rudolph Fisher; first, that he knows how to build up and to contrast characters; second, that he knows from the inside the various classes that compose the Harlem milieu; and, third, that he is a good craftsman.

These elements come to the fore in *The Walls of Jericho*. Here is a cross-section of Harlem showing every stratum of society and every shade of color from white and those who pass for white, through yellow, yellow-brown, chocolate and black. The story shows up the stormy relations of these groups with each other. Shine, the young hero, is a piano mover of prodigious size and strength. This book did not resort to the sensationalism that has given the public such a distorted picture of the black metropolis. A reviewer in the *Saturday Review of Literature* was favorably impressed with Mr. Fisher's ability to vivify and delineate character:

> Jinks and Bubber, the Damon and Pythias of Harlem, yet continually quarrelling, are two of the most delightful colored characters our fiction has yet given rise to.[11]

His graphic and quiet style was at its best in describing the tempestuous courtship of Shine and Linda, and Fisher unfolded the story beautifully.[12] A London critic thought there were four cardinal qualities in this distinctive novel: its vigour, its humor, its satire, and its charm[13]; and undoubtedly this story teller was able to hold the reader's attention from first to last and his style had reached that stage of artistic development where art produces the illusion of naturalness.

Mr. Fisher died on December 26, 1935, and thus the Harlem Renaissance lost one of its most brilliant figures, a man who told stories because he was an artist in love with life and with words.

11. *Saturday Review of Literature,* Vol. 5, p. 100 (September 8, 1928).
12. *Saturday Review,* Vol. 146, p. 250 (August 25, 1928).
13. *London Spectator,* Vol. 141, p. 252 (August 25, 1928).

Chapter 9

Jessie Fauset

Her Life

Jessie Fauset was born at Show Hill, New Jersey. After graduating from the public schools of Philadelphia, she completed her formal education at Cornell University and the University of Pennsylvania. Her Phi Beta Kappa key was received from Cornell University. For several years she taught Latin and French in the Dunbar High School in Washington, D.C., and later she served as literary editor of the *Crisis*. At the present time Miss Fauset is teaching in New York City.

Perhaps the fact that she is the daughter of a minister and was reared in a conventional home channeled the course that she was to follow in her depiction of the Negro life in the upper classes. Undoubtedly the fact that she became an ardent worker in the National Association for the Advancement of Colored People, an organization dedicated to the proposition that Negroes can achieve their rights through agitational efforts, made her a disciple of what Dr. W.E.B. Du Bois has called "the talented tenth." T. S. Stribling's *Birthright,* a novel that pictured the disintegration of a Harvard Negro, made Miss Fauset very angry; and she determined to write books that would show the brighter side of Negro life. It is this obsessing preoccupation with the foibles and psychoses of the dark bourgeoisie that led Mr. H. L. Mencken to say in a private conversation: "The characters of Jessie Fauset need some chittlings in their mouths." The Southern peon likes the intestines of hogs, chittlings or chitterlings. This was Mr.

Mencken's way of saying that Jessie Fauset's characters were too stiff and waxlike, patterned too much after Emily Post.*

Her Travels

Jessie Fauset has traveled extensively in England, Scotland, France, Belgium, Switzerland, Italy, Austria, and Algeria, for she is one of the "Veiled Aristocrats" whose sophistication she delights in etching.[1] As she made her way leisurely through these countries, she sent neat accounts to the *Crisis,* articles that revealed her observations of scenes and customs reminding one of those sent to the *Tribune* by that other intellectual woman of a bygone period, Margaret Fuller.

Her use of the spoken French, the French of the Parisian, was improved in the Alliance Française and the Guilde Internationale, and she lingered at the College de France, absorbing its atmosphere of classicism. She put this to use as the interpreter of the Second Pan-African Congress in Paris and as a teacher of French in New York.[2] Dancing, cards, and the theater afford her recreation when she is not teaching French, writing lyrics, or creating portraits of the cultivated Negro of her Philadelphia milieu.

---

* [Tolson's attitude towards Fauset was revealed in "Candid Camera Shots of Negro Intellectuals," June 29, 1940. It reads in part: "I shall write my study of Jessie Fauset without interviewing her. In fact, I know now all that I need know about her. I see now why the characters in her books are so stilted and unreal. She is always trying to prove that Negroes know Emily Post." Quoted in Farnsworth, *Caviar and Cabbage,* p. 256.]

1. Gertrude Sanborn, *Veiled Aristocrats,* Washington, D.C., Associated Publishers, 1924. [For commentary of Fauset's relationship to the renaissance, see George Hutchinson, *The Harlem Renaissance in Black and White,* 156–57; David Levering Lewis, *When Harlem Was in Vogue,* 121–25; and Nathan Huggins, *Harlem Renaissance,* 146–48.]
2. Countee Cullen, *Caroling Dusk,* New York, Harper, 1927, p. 65. [Cullen does not comment on her role as translator.]

Four Panels of the Veiled Aristocrats

The first panel in Jessie Fauset's veiled aristocrats was called *There is Confusion.*[3] It is the story of the Marshalls, wealthy and ambitious, of the daughter Joanna, seeking fame in the realm of music, of her love for Peter Bye, cursed with the drug of laziness. It was hailed as the "first work of fiction to come from the pen of a colored woman in these United States."[4]

Dr. James Weldon Johnson pointed out the lightness and neatness of her touch, the same touch which she shows in "the *vers de société* that she has written."[5] Another critic saw in *There is Confusion* the artistic hand of a novelist who recalled the objective impersonality of the woman who wrote *The House of Mirth* and *The Age of Innocence:*

> She possesses the critical insight and resolute detachment of the novelist, and her picture of the society which her novel surveys is achieved with an art as impersonal as that of Mrs. Wharton.[6]

The second panel in Miss Fauset's series was *Plum Bun.*[7] It is the story of Angela Morgan, an educated colored girl fair enough to pass for white. The question of "passing" has intrigued a large number of novelists both white and black, for it holds so many dramatic possibilities.[8] Angela Morgan, changing her name, goes to New York City to live in Greenwich Village, and embarks on an unhappy love affair with a white man. Her younger sister, who is unmistakably Negro, also goes to New York, but lives in Harlem, and the sisters rarely meet. Anthony Cross—the ancient makeshift of selecting a name to emphasize a situation[9]—enters the lives of both, but he does not know that they are sisters. He too is "passing."

---

3. Jessie Fauset, *There is Confusion,* New York, Boni & Liveright, 1924.
4. *New Republic,* [by E. D. W.] Vol. 39, p. 192 (July 9, 1924).
5. James Weldon Johnson, *The Book of American Negro Poetry,* p. 205.
6. *Independent Book Review,* Vol. 13, p. 48 (June 24, 1924).
7. Jessie Fauset, *Plum Bun,* New York, Stokes, 1929.
8. Mark Twain, *Pudd'nhead Wilson,* New York, Harper, 1899.
9. James Knapp Reeves, *The Writer's Book,* Cincinnati, Writer's Digest, 1938, p. 123.

Undoubtedly Miss Fauset used this fortuitous coincidence to escape from the solution of a difficult problem. From Edward Sheldon's *The Nigger*[10] to Clement Wood's *Nigger*[11] novelists have tantalized readers with this interracial dilemma and extricated their baffled characters by a *deus ex machina.* Of course, Maxwell Bodenheim's *Ninth Avenue* was an exception.[12]

Jessie Fauset has had some difficulty in getting publishers, who are in the business for money and not art, to bring out her novels. They say that people in the large do not understand books that deal with Negroes of the upper class; such veiled aristocrats seem improbable to the white reading public. So it appears that Miss Fauset has a narrow chance of achieving her ambition of writing a best seller. Accordingly, the third panel *The Chinaberry Tree*[13] did not gain publication until it was given a very fine introduction by Miss Zona Gale, a sincere friend of the Harlem Renaissance. This story deals with the private lives of colored Americans untouched by any but very casual contacts with whites, and the narrative centers about two cousins tainted by illegitimacy.

Again Jessie Fauset showed her basic interest was situational, but in her fine analyses of her characters she revealed the "work of a remarkable psychologist."[14] While the novel contained nothing of the lurid sensationalism of *Infants of the Spring*[15] and the picturesque caricatures of *This Side of Jordan,*[16] aspects of Negro life exploited by most novelists, it was certainly more illuminating. If there was a noticeable weakness in the work, it was to be found in the too romantic figure of Laurentine. Of all the Harlem writers, Jessie Fauset is the most persistent delineator of what Dr. Alain Locke delights in calling "The New Negro."

The fourth novel in the panel of the veiled aristocrats was named *Comedy: American Style,*[17] a story of a group of near-white colored people liv-

10. Edward Sheldon, *The Nigger,* New York, Macmillan, 1910.
11. Clement Wood, *Nigger,* New York, Dutton, 1922.
12. Maxwell Bodenheim, *Ninth Avenue,* New York, Boni & Liveright, 1926.
13. Jessie Fauset, *The Chinaberry Tree,* New York, Stokes, 1932.
14. *Nation,* Vol. 135, p. 88 (July 27, 1932).
15. Wallace Thurman, *Infants of the Spring,* New York, Macauley, 1932.
16. Roark Bradford, *This Side of Jordan,* New York, Harper, 1929.
17. Jessie Fauset, *Comedy: American Style,* New York, Stokes, 1933.

ing in Philadelphia, and of the tragedies which resulted from the short-sightedness of one woman who herself insisted on "passing" and tried to force her husband and children to do likewise. The way the title sounded the theme of the book, the strength of the plot and the arresting situations, caused one critic to affirm:

> The title is well chosen for a country where the presence of blond Negroes gives an especially ironic emphasis to the comedy of racial purity.[18]

In her four panels of the dusky upper classes, Miss Fauset displays a wealth of observation and experience, telling her stories with an intellectual objectivity; and Mr. Harlan Hatcher sums up the novels in the following ways:

> Unlike most the stories of the common Negroes where the interest is in social conditions and the characters are only types which could be moved from one book to another with little disturbance, these novels are concerned with psychology, motivations, and the life of a cultivated people with intellectual interests.[19]

Miss Fauset is caught on the horns of a dilemma like one of her bewildered characters. She is a passionate crusader for Dr. Du Bois's "Talented Tenth" in America. She wants to reach a wide audience with her panels of the veiled aristocrats. But the intellectual austerity of her delineations, for the present at least, sets up a perpendicular barrier between her and the object of her ardent quest. She probably has fewer readers among her own people than any other member of the Harlem group, and her white public consists of a small segment of the intelligentsia. The vagabond Langston Hughes singing his "Weary Blues," chanting of life in "a nigger place," captivates audiences wherever he goes and gains a host of dusky readers, while Miss Jessie Fauset languishes in her intellectual solitude.

---

18. *Nation,* Vol. 138, p. 26 (January 3, 1934).
19. Harlan Hatcher, *Creating the Modern American Novel,* p. 151.

Chapter 10

George Schuyler

His Life

George Schuyler, satirist, columnist, novelist, and editor, was born in Providence, Rhode Island, in 1895; and, after his parents had settled in Syracuse, New York, he was educated in the public schools of that city.[1] His grandmother, on his father's side, was a princess from Madagascar, who was either stolen or bought by a Dutch sea-captain and taken to Rotterdam, Holland. Evidently she was not a slave there, but served as an apprentice. The custom of apprenticeship was quite common even among those of African blood during that period. later she was brought to America and came into the possession of the famous Schuyler family of New York, at the age of eighteen.

On both sides of the family there is the German influence, and undoubtedly something of this finds expression in George Schuyler's love for the pragmatic. His bourgeois enemies have called him the Black Mencken, with scorn in their voices. The fact is, however, that George

1. V. F. Calverton, *Anthology of American Negro Literature,* p. 534. [For a good overview of Schuyler's work see Michael Peplow, *George S. Schuyler.* Also of interest is Henry Louis Gates, Jr., "A Fragmented Man: George S. Schuyler and Claims of Race."]

Schuyler was writing satire in the United States army, caricaturing his superior officers before he had ever heard of Mencken.

At sixteen years of age Schuyler joined the regular army, and served for six years, attaining the rank of the first lieutenant. While in the Hawaiian Islands he did four things of a literary nature: read philosophy, economics, and literature, wrote for a white daily in Honolulu, organized the Scott Literary Society among his hard-boiled comrades, and wrote satires and fables dealing with army life. The satires got under the skin of his superior officers and Schuyler's popular bulletin was banned in the camp.

George Schuyler is the arch foe of class snobbishness and a fearless defender of the underdog. Perhaps his own habits of life have had a great deal to do with this attitude. He knows the pang of hunger and the feel of uncompanionable city streets during the dawn hours. He has dragged his weary feet from Harlem to the Bowery to get a free lunch. He has slept many a night in Central Park with dirty newspapers for a pillow.

Mr. Schuyler told the writer that on one occasion when he was down to fifty cents he bought fifty postal cards and then secured fifty addresses from a city directory. To these he mailed the postal cards asking for a chance to do any kind of work. He received six replies, and from these he made a selection of one of the jobs.

During these years of poverty and public indifference, he was reading extensively and writing short articles. The story goes that once he worked for a great inventor whose wife was beautiful but very ignorant. Schuyler read all the books in the private library of his boss, and then he and the inventor used to hide away upstairs to discuss philosophy while the wife entertained her noisy friends at the bridge table.

When quite a young man Schuyler became a member of the Socialist Party in Syracuse, and in that city he had a running editorial fight with the editor of the *Syracuse Herald.* In 1926 Schuyler became the assistant editor of the *Messenger,* a radical New York journal. However, he left that position because of a difference concerning the editorial policy of the magazine, and in 1928 he was made manager of the W. B. Ziff Syndicate in Chicago, With that company Schuyler did all types of writing, from articles on current social and economic questions to confession stories. The prosperity of the company increased and Schuyler's salary rose as the months passed. But he was not doing the things that he wanted to do, and his dissatisfaction grew apace.[2]

Finally Mrs. Schuyler urged her husband to try his journalistic fortunes in New York. Coming East, he secured a position as columnist with the *Pittsburgh Courier,* the Negro weekly which has the largest circulation in the United States. For many years Schuyler has been hailed as the best of the Negro columnists. His iconoclastic articles have become quite popular, and he has many disciples from Harlem to Waycross, Georgia, whose tenets are violently opposed by the Negro conservatives. Negro readers had not seen a pen like that of George Schuyler's: it was daring, biting, unanswerable. Dr. Du Bois had been thought radical; but, nevertheless, he did respect the middle-class virtues. Schuyler's radicalism, on the other hand, centered its attack on these mores dear to the soul of dark respectability. The Negro clergy and the caste system within the race did not escape venomous assaults. Schuyler sneered at the so-called progress of the race. He ripped open the inhibitions and complexes of "Big Niggers."

But he was fair with his opponents. He published the scathing letters he received every week and countered with irrefutable logic. Nobody need doubt where Schuyler stood on anything. His articles were a regular feature of the *American Mercury* under the editorship of Mr. Mencken. Prejudiced whites could not understand this Negro who simply laughed at their vaunted superiority and pointed out their ridiculosities. Mr. Mencken received letters from all parts of the South, and he and Schuyler enjoyed them immensely. One white woman from South Carolina wrote Schuyler if he ever came to that state she would see that he was lynched by Southern chivalry. Schuyler was lecturing in the state at that particular time. This was one of many threats.

George Schuyler has written the most outstanding satire on the race problem in the United States; at least this is the opinion of Mr. V. F. Calverton in his notable introduction to the *Anthology of American Negro Literature,* the standard work on the subject in many colleges and universities.[3]

---

2. Footnote: This biographical material was given the writer by Mrs. George Schuyler.
3. V. F. Calverton, *Anthology of American Negro Literature,* p. 14.

George Schuyler has waged an incessant war with the *Negro World,* the official organ of Marcus Garvey, leader of the sensational Back-to-Africa Movement, which in the period of its barbaric splendor, renting Madison Square Garden for a whole month to hold its international congress, its membership was larger than that of any other Negro movement in history. Said the oracular *Negro World:*

> It is easier for a camel to go through the eye of a needle than it is for George Schuyler to refrain from wallowing in the gutter.[4]

George Schuyler has a unique vocabulary of colorful terms dealing with both races, as pointed out by the *Baltimore Afro-American:*

> For Negro: colored, Aframerican, sooty brethren, Ethiop, shine, blackamoor, Senagambian, dark brother, Negro, chocolate, moke, smoke, Uncle Tom, coon, and Sambo; for whites: Nordic, cracker, peckerwood, Anglo-Saxon, ofay, rednecks, pork-skin, and Caucasian.[5]

Schuyler's method of attack daunts his most stubborn enemies, for the dignity which it is necessary to assume becomes the target, the easy target, of the satirist. A New York periodical gave a very clear picture of Schuyler going into battle:

> He asks and gives no quarter. A master of words, he is building up for himself a wall of bitterness. Schuyler's method of dissecting his victim is unique. He spares no words. His thoughts are sharp as a two-edged sword.[6]

Another critic points out the nature of the elements that have given his style effectiveness:

> His clean-cut, biting style inevitably in keeping with his theme and purpose is at times superb. He meets his materials with a directness that com-

4. *Negro World,* New York, Vol. V., p. 8 (September 3, 1927).
5. *Baltimore Afro-American,* Vol. 25, p. 16 (December 3, 1927).
6. *America's News,* Vol. 8, p. 10 (August 20, 1927).

> pels by its vigor. His writing is never sentimental; rather, it has a hard, metallic brilliance that convinces without endeavoring to caress.[7]

And yet one who has read Schuyler's articles and books is compelled to agree with the writer of the following interpretation, who sees into the soul of this black Diogenes, yes, who has probed beneath the tough surface of the satire that covers the real George Schuyler:

> Schuyler is an idealistic materialist, a whirlwind in the midst of a muddy world. He is a man alone. He is neither a "New Negro" nor an "Old One."[8]

Black No More[9]

In *Black No More,* George Schuyler concentrated the various elements of his temperament and craftsmanship on the production of a satire which dealt with the subject of color and race prejudice in the United States, bringing into the foreground the comedy and tragedy, the inconsistency and paradox, that obtain in the theory and practice of *bi-racialism.*

In this satire Dr. Crookman discovers a depigmentation process by which, overnight, a black may become a veritable blond. Since his fees are small, depending on mass production and mass distribution, in a short while the whole Negro population rapidly turn white, change names, and intermarry with the whites. When the colored babies come, Dr. Crookman bleaches them in lying-in hospitals. In time the blonds begin to suffer the same prejudices hitherto placed upon the blacks; and people dye their skins dark in order to achieve a new, exclusive race distinction of a brown complexion.

It is obvious that the journalist Schuyler put his tale together with that haste so noticeable in the work of Walter White; yet "it is a challenging idea, developed with almost savage gusto."[10] While the satirist has made

---

7. V. F. Calverton, *op. cit.*, p. 14.
8. *America's News, Ibid.*, p. 10.
9. George Schuyler, *Black No More,* New York, Macauley, 1931. [See Jane Kuenz, "American Racial Discourse, 1900–1930: Schuyler's *Black No More.*"]
10. *Survey,* Vol. 66, p. 290 (June 1, 1931).

every white character a hypocrite in the story, on the other hand, all the Negroes are knaves, even those that are most blatant in their aims to elevate the dark masses,[11] and there is little doubt that the book was "a very pointed barb in the side of black and white alike."[12]

Perhaps in this book George Schuyler is very much the elephant in the china shop, and "goes bludgeoning his way through it, striking down right and left the strawmen it has set up."[13] Schuyler has the zeal of a crusader as he sallies forth against the exploiters of our most popular prejudice. He lays it on with a trowel, so to speak, and the response calls for a big guffaw.

Slaves Today[14]

Slaves Today was the result of a trip that Schuyler made to Liberia, the Negro republic on the West Coast of Africa. It deals with the twentieth-century slave trade that is carried on by American corporations and Liberian officials in the exploitation of the natives. In no other work is the burning idealism of George Schuyler seen to better advantage, for this book suggests the manner of *Uncle Tom's Cabin.*[15]

Although one is amazed at the degradation of those simple tribes and the background has all the lure of the unfamiliar and the bizarre, nothing of sentimentality enters his work[16]; it is, in fact, a book belonging to the recent American school often called "the hard-boiled."[17] It is a simple and unadorned story showing a stage of human suffering unsurpassed for poignancy and sorrow when one considers the fact that these African

11. *Bookman,* Vol. 72, p. 8 (February 1931).
12. Dorothy Van Doren, "George Schuyler, Satirist," *Nation,* Vol. 132, p. 218 (February 25, 1931).
13. *Saturday Review of Literature,* Vol. 7, p. 799 (May 2, 1931).
14. George Schuyler, *Slaves Today,* New York, Harcourt & Brace, 1932.
15. *American Mercury,* Vol. 25, p. 26 (February 1932).
16. *America's News,* Vol. 8, p. 10 (August 20, 1931).
17. Harlan Hatcher, *Creating the Modern American Novel,* p. 255. [Tolson is referring to the chapter title, "Poetic Versus Hard-Boiled Realism."]

natives have become the victims of the ruling class of Liberia, enslaved by members of the same race whose ancestors had been slaves themselves.[18]

Meanwhile, George Schuyler, the exulting satirist, continues his hunting, bow and poisoned darts in hand, and here and there one discovers some sham or hypocrisy that he has slain.

18. V. F. Calverton, *op. cit.*, p. 14. [The citation is not correct. Calverton refers here to *Our Greatest Gift to America.*]

Chapter 11

William Edward Burghardt Du Bois

His Life

William Du Bois was born in 1868 at Great Barrington, Massachusetts. He grew up in the Puritan atmosphere and culture of old New England, and since there were few Negroes in the town it was not until his young manhood that he became familiar with the people of his own race. In *Dark Water*[1] he has given to the world one of the significant autobiographies of our time, for in that book he has recorded in his beautiful poetic prose the soul-experiences of a dark youth in whom there was the unleap of genius and how the dusky wings of his spirit beat against the bars of prejudice. He was educated at Fisk University, Harvard University, and the University of Berlin.[2]

In an address at Columbia University, in the Horace Mann Auditorium, on March 30, 1932, Dr. Du Bois related many of the things that featured [sic] his life during his academic career. His contacts with the aboli-

1. W. E. B. Du Bois, *Dark Water,* New York, Harcourt & Brace, 1920.
2. "Biographical Sketches," *Readings from Negro Authors,* Cromwell, Turner, and Dykes, editors, p. 366. [For an excellent general study of Du Bois, see Arnold Rampersad, *The Art and Imagination of W. E. B. Du Bois.*]

tionist teachers at Fisk University fired him with a desire to elevate his people and to reveal to the world their thought-life. For over forty years of public service he has not swerved from his lofty purpose. No one who is familiar with the work of Dr. Du Bois can deny that he has done herculean service in opposing the advance of race prejudice and intolerance in the United States.

At different times he has served as a teacher at Wilberforce University, the University of Pennsylvania, and Atlanta University, and this year the last-named institution is holding a mammoth anniversary celebration in his honor.[3]

Du Bois and the Atlanta Compromise

The address of Booker T. Washington at the Atlanta Exposition in 1895 marked the beginning of an epoch and the end of an era in the history of the race problem in America.[4] The young sage of Tuskegee came forward and harmonized the North, the South, and the Negro by advocating for the blacks a policy of industrial education. He denied by a subtle, but an unmistakable, implication that the Negro wanted social and political equality. This had been the red flag that had inflamed the South since the Reconstruction Period, and, with these concessions made, the South was pacified. The white North, anxious to get rid of a perplexing problem, welcomed the Atlanta Compromise with gushing enthusiasm.

But in Atlanta University there was a young professor of economics and history who saw with mixed amazement and indignation this sacrifice of the Negro's constitutional rights. The result was a book which is still significant to students and critics. It was called the *Souls of Black Folk.*[5] Into it young Du Bois poured his scholarship and his soul, and it became a classic in the literature of its type. It contains that remarkable short narrative "The Passing of the First Born," in which Du Bois tells about the sorrowful loss of his little son and then the "awful gladness" that came to him

3. *Pittsburgh Courier*, Vol. XXVIII, p. 24 (March 5, 1938).
4. James Weldon Johnson, *Black Manhattan*, p. 138.
5. W. E. B. Du Bois, *Souls of Black Folk*, Chicago, McClurg, 1903.

when he realized that the child has escaped from the color bars that would have bruised and deformed his spirit. Mary White Ovington tells of a young man who struggled to read this story aloud; then, sobbing, how he threw the book across the room and swore: "No man should dare to write like that!"[6]

America grew conscious of a dusky genius who wrote in a limpid prose unexcelled by any other writer in the language; and Professor William James, his old Harvard teacher, in those earlier years of his student career, marvelled at the youth's beauty of expression.[7] Moreover, even Booker T. Washington writhed under the lash of his satire and caustic wit.[8] This book made Du Bois the unquestioned leader of the radical group of Negro intellectuals. While it is true that his Harvard dissertation on *The Suppression of the African Slave Trade*[9] had established him as a scholar, it is equally true that he had no appreciable following in his race.

Du Bois, the Organizer

Du Bois has been a man of action as well as a man of thought. First came the Niagara Movement, which was an abortive attempt to concentrate the agitation of Negro and White intellectuals for a united attack on Dr. Washington's Atlanta Compromise; and this was followed by his being appointed Director of Publicity for the National Association for the Advancement of Colored People.[10] He also became the editor of the *Crisis*, a magazine which has exerted a powerful influence. Working with liberal whites, the Association has been the most potent single factor in fighting race prejudice and segregation in the United States.

---

6. Mary White Ovington, *Portraits in Color*, p. 79.
7. Kelly Miller, *The New York Amsterdam News*, Vol. XVI, p. 15 (April 13, 1932).
8. Carter G. Woodson, *The Negro in Our History*, Washington, D.C., Associated Publishers, 1922, p. 487.
9. W. E. B. Du Bois, *The Suppression of the African Slave Trade*, Cambridge, Harvard University Press, 1896.
10. Carter G. Woodson, *Ibid.*, p. 487.

> It sprang from the whites and blacks who believed that some good could be accomplished by publicity, by agitation, and by memorializing the State Legislatures and Congress for the redress of these grievances.[11]

Later, Du Bois met Marcus Garvey, the most glamorous figure that has ever risen in Afro-American history. Marcus Garvey had come from the West Indies with a plan for the solution of the Negro problem in the Americas.

The soil was fertile for the seeds of chauvinism. Thousands of Negro soldiers were returning from the Western Front where they had fought to make the world safe for democracy and—in the eloquent words of Colonel Roscoe Simmons—"Georgia safe for a black man." Reports had already come to the black masses that black boys had been mistreated "Over There" by their fellow Americans. When the colored soldiers returned, it was discovered from their own lips that the earlier rumors had been true.

Then followed a series of race riots in Houston, Longview, Chicago, East St. Louis, and in other places. A Negro was beaten to death in front of the White House, and the President was silent.[12] His rhetorical statement "the world must be made safe for democracy" became irony that poisoned the minds of the black masses.

It was during this period that Claude McKay fused the elements of fear and bitterness and desperation in his sonnet, "If We Must Die." This poem, striking the first revolutionary note in American Negro history, was published in Harlem and reprinted in scores of Negro newspapers. It became a sort of rallying cry.

At this psychological moment Marcus Garvey walked upon the scene, as if destiny had signalled his entrance. The stage was all set for his fantastic Back-To-Africa Movement. Tens of thousands entered his organization. Remote parts of the world were touched by his influence. The African possessions of France and Great Britain grew restive, and the two major powers in Europe became alarmed. Secret agents followed the every word and act of the self-styled His Excellency, the Provisional President of Africa, surrounded by His Highness's Knight-Commanders of the

11. Carter G. Woodson, *op. cit.*, p. 487.
12. James Weldon Johnson, *Black Manhattan*, p. 264. [The citation is a reference to Claude McKay.]

Distinguished Order of Ethiopia, Knight-Commanders of the Sublime Order of the Nile, with their court etiquette, gorgeous regalia, decorations, and insignia.[13]

Dr. Du Bois had been planning for months to enter the arena, and the result was the launching of his Pan-African Congress in 1917. He hoped to "establish some common meeting ground and unity of thought among the Negro peoples of the whole world through biennial meetings."[14] Here was an answer to the fantastic arguments of Garveyism, it seemed to Dr. Du Bois. But Garvey was his own undoing. In a wild burst of enthusiasm, he bought a palace in Harlem, gave lucrative positions to black dukes and barons, and appointed high-salaried generals for imaginary African armies. He held vociferous mass meetings in Carnegie Hall, stormed Madison Square Garden with uniformed delegates from all corners of the world, purchased discarded government ships and placed on them black sailors who knew little about nautical things. He rode in regal splendor through Harlem and held high court in a manner comparable to that of an oriental potentate; and at night His African Highness and his royal followers repaired to Liberty Hall, where the Provisional President of Africa swayed the black multitude with the wand of his golden oratory. Then came the collapse, sudden, melodramatic, and inevitable; and Marcus Garvey, bewildered, suffering from delusions of persecution, found himself behind the austere walls of Atlanta federal prison, for defrauding his credulous disciples through the use of the United States mails.

Circumstances, in the form of Marcus Garvey's bizarre program for the black millions, again left Dr. Du Bois the undisputed champion of the dark cosmos, and his Pan-African Movement grew at the expense of the disintegration of Marcus Garvey's Back-to-Africa Movement. Thirteen countries were represented in the 1922 meeting held in London.[15]

---

13. Mary White Ovington, *op. cit.*, pp. 23–24.
14. Carter G. Woodson, *op. cit.*, p. 554.
15. Carter G. Woodson, *op. cit.*, p. 554. [For comments on the relationship between Du Bois and Garvey see David Levering Lewis, *When Harlem Was in Vogue*, 37, 42, 44.]

His Attitude Toward Race Literature

Dr. Du Bois is venomous in attacking anything that may have an unfavorable effect on his people; therefore, any writer, black or white, who depicts Negro low-life, is in for a lambasting at his hands, whether the novelist is a Carl Van Vechten with a *Nigger Heaven* or a Wallace Thurman with a proletarian drama like *Harlem*. Holding the theory that literature is propagandistic and scornful of the art for art's sake rationalization, Dr. Du Bois maintains that the literature of the race should be clean and ennobling. Realists and naturalists of the modern hard-boiled school are usually the objects of his uncompromising attacks, and he satirizes them pitilessly.[16]

An American Tragedy

The fact that Dr. Du Bois has sacrificed himself for his racial principles has caused many critics to look upon him as an American tragedy. They say that an artist has been placed on the pyre of propaganda, one who had in him the genius to produce masterpieces that would have transcended race in the universality of their appeal.

In 1932 Dr. Kelly Miller, dean of Howard University, lamented in a conversation that the Negro had lost literary works of supreme merit because Dr. Du Bois had busied himself with a passing phase of American life; the verve of *Souls of Black Folk* had sold itself for the dubious gains of ethnic expediency. Wallace Thurman, editor, novelist, and critic, says:

> He is one of the outstanding men of this or any other generation. He has served his race well; so well, in fact, that the artist in him has been stifled in order that the propagandist might live.[17]

---

16. W. E. B. Du Bois, "The Negro Mind Reaches Out," *The New Negro*, edited by Alain Locke, New York, Albert & Charles Boni, 1925, pp. 385–414. [For a discussion of Du Bois's ideas on race see Kwame Anthony Appiah, "The Conservation of 'Race.'"]
17. Wallace Thurman, "High, Low, Past and Present," *Harlem*, Vol. 1, p. 31 (November 1928).

The Gift of Black Folk[18]

In 1924 Dr. Du Bois brought out a history that revealed the contributions of the Negro to civilization. It was a scholarly piece of work in which he showed "the gift of style and polemic."[19] It swept the reader along at a breathless pace and possessed much of the dramatic narrative of a moving novel. Dr. Du Bois always presents his case with fairness and logical coherence, even though his style is often veined with cynicism and satire.[20]

It is strange, yet true, that his propaganda is more clearly enunciated in his novels than in his historical documents. In the latter he shows what Dr. Denung used to call the prerequisites of the great historian: stern accuracy in the presentation of facts and a bold imagination in the construction of the milieu and the characters depicted. Dr. Du Bois, a literary historian, has given his contemporaries a book which demolishes myths and inspires a sympathetic understanding of certain traditions that bewilder and plague his countrymen.

The Dark Princess[21]

In that novel *The Quest of the Silver Fleece*[22] Du Bois had written a book which Dr. Alain Locke thought should be placed on a shelf with Frank Norris' fiction, because of its significant accomplishment in making "Cotton the great protagonist of fate in the lives of the Southern people, both black and white."[23]

In *The Dark Princess* Du Bois started out as if he were gong to write a great American novel in the objective style. His hero is a Negro medical student in a New York university whose mother is putting him through school. He is about to take up hospital practice when he encounters the hydra of race prejudice. Disgusted, he leaves America. The chapters depict-

18. W. E. B. Du Bois, *Gift of Black Folk*, Boston, Stratford, 1924.
19. *Bookman*, Vol. 60, p. 357 (November 1924).
20. *Survey*, Vol. 59, p. 164 (November 1, 1924).
21. W. E. B. Du Bois, *The Dark Princess*, New York, Harcourt & Brace, 1928.
22. W. E. B. Du Bois, *The Quest of the Silver Fleece*, Chicago, McClurg, 1911.
23. Alain Locke, *The New Negro*, p. 43.

ing the young man's life as it contacts the motley derelicts in the galleys are done with vivid unsentimentality. One begins to realize that here is realism at its best.

Then with an abruptness that is disconcerting, Dr. Du Bois, the propagandist, rushes upon the scene, and we find the hero plunged with miraculous immediacy into the tangle of Dr. Du Bois' own beloved Pan-African Congress under the guise of a proposed unification of the Darker Races.

Finally, disappointed, the hero reaches Chicago and enters the labyrinthine world of politics on the South Side. Again, Du Bois does excellent work in the objective form. Soon, however, he remembers that the Unity of the Dark Races—the eminent Doctor's favorite pet nowadays—had been ignored too long; so the Indian Princess—the great scholar has a literary weakness for dusky women—bobs up out of nowhere, and the book ends in a fantastic maze of metaphysical and sociological speculations as far removed from reality as the illusions of a Hindu mystic. All of which caused Jane Reitell to say:

> The book is an amazing mixture of fact and fancy. The black man's burden of suffering is a cross which sometimes must be borne on the shoulders of humanity.[24]

Rising above the laments on the tragedy of Dr. Du Bois' prostitution of his art, came the voice of a critic in the *World Tomorrow,* a magazine whose very name suggests its purpose; this writer considered the novel "a piece of symbolic social literature and propaganda written with fine nervous ardor and scorn for injustice."[25]

Black Reconstruction[26]

The title explains the nature of Dr. Du Bois' latest book. It is written in the light of economic determinism and upsets most of the current ideas con-

24. Jane Reitell, "Black Reconstruction," *Annals American Academy,* Vol. 140, p. 347 (November 1928).
25. *World Tomorrow,* Vol. II, p. 473 (November 1928).
26. W. E. B. Du Bois, *Black Reconstruction,* New York, Harcourt & Brace, 1935.

cerning the roles of the Negroes and the Yankees in the reconstruction of the South. The book created a furor. Professor Henry Raymond Mussey said in an interview for the New York *Herald-Tribune* on July 1, 1925:

> It is an economic treatise, a philosophical discussion, an impassioned argument for the thesis so ably and eloquently maintained by its author over a generation, a poem, a work of art, all rolled into one.
>
> No intelligent person can read this book without profound respect for the scholarship of its author, in plowing a solitary furrow in an unbroken field.

Mr. Floyd J. Calvin, after making a survey of the critical comments on Dr. Du Bois' latest work, released the following statements through his syndicated column:

> The battle still rages over Dr. W. E. B. Du Bois' *Black Reconstruction*. . . . The forthright denunciation of several celebrated white historians, whom Dr. Du Bois called by name in his famous "Blacklist" included in the bibliography of the monumental work has brought apologetic replies.[27]

Dr. Du Bois has left the editor's chair and returned to that of the professor at Atlanta University, the place where he wrote his first book, *The Souls of Black Folk*.

For the first time in its history, the National Association for the Advancement of Colored People held its annual meeting without him, in St. Louis during the summer of 1935. Editor J. Alston of a noted Southern paper commented that the absence of the old scholar's dynamic personality left a void in the organization that evoked the pathetic.[28]

Only the literary critic of the future will be able to answer Wallace Thurman's question: Was Dr. Du Bois justified in laying aside the pen of the artist to take up the bludgeon of the propagandist?

---

27. Floyd J. Calvin, "Dr. W. E. B. Du Bois," *Pittsburgh Courier*, Vol. XXV, p. 10 (July 6, 1935).
28. J. Alston, "The N.A.A.C.P.," *Houston Informer*, Vol. XX, p. 6 (July 13, 1935).

Chapter 12

James Weldon Johnson

His Life

James Weldon Johnson was born June 17, 1871, at Jacksonville, Florida. He attended the public schools of his native city, and then went up to Atlanta University in Atlanta, Georgia, from which he received his B.A. in 1894. For several years he served as principal of the high school, which he built into a first-class educational center for the people of the surrounding region. Education for Negroes in Florida, at that time, was not a very popular thing. In 1897 he was admitted to the bar, and Jacksonville became the sphere of his legal, as well as his academic, activities.[1] In that Southern atmosphere he passed through many of the experiences which he later put into his famous *The Autobiography of an Ex-Colored Man.*[2]

In collaboration with his distinguished brother, J. Rosamond Johnson, pianist and arranger of Negro spirituals, James Weldon Johnson wrote an operetta for their own entertainment. James Weldon did the lyrics and the

1. Stanley J. Kunitz, *Living Authors,* p. 197. [For a general overview of his work see Robert E. Fleming, *James Weldon Johnson* (1987). Johnson's influence on the renaissance is discussed in David Levering Lewis, *When Harlem Was in Vogue,* 143–49, and in Cary D. Wintz, *Black Culture and the Harlem Renaissance,* 102–12.]
2. James Weldon Johnson, *The Autobiography of an Ex-Colored Man,* New York, Sherman & French, 1912.

libretto, and Rosamond composed the music. In 1901 the brothers came to New York City with the manuscript and attempted to sell it on Broadway. They did not succeed, but the contacts that were formed led to future emoluments.

A product of this period of collaboration was the Negro national anthem, "Lift Every Voice and Sing,"[3] which brought the brothers a great vogue. Churches, schools, and colleges took up the stirring air and sang it on important occasions throughout the country.

In 1904 James Weldon Johnson received his M.A. from Atlanta University, and later he did graduate study at Columbia University for three years, receiving much encouragement in his creative work from that seasoned scholar, Professor Brander Mathews, to whom Johnson pays a fine tribute of appreciation in his widely acclaimed autobiography *Along This Way.*[4] During this period he gained a mastery of literary forms and contacted many of the Harlem characters whose lives he was to portray in his *Black Manhattan.*[5] He was sent to Corinto, Nicaragua, where he became a spectator of the Zelaya revolution and witnessed the abortive attempt to overthrow Diaz. He rendered valuable services to his country by protecting the interests and properties of Americans. In South America he perfected his knowledge of Spanish, and this enabled him to make his way as a careful translator during his career in New York City.

In 1910 he married Grace Nail of New York City. Living in the metropolis, he translated the English libretto of *Goyescas* and the Spanish opera was produced by the Metropolitan Opera Company in 1915.[6] During his less fortunate days the great Oscar Hammerstein had climbed the rickety stairs of his dilapidated dwelling to hear his comic-opera.

He had brought with him from South America the manuscript of *The Autobiography of an Ex-Colored Man,* and in 1912 he succeeded in getting a publisher and the book appeared anonymously; but in 1927 it was reissued under his own name. Furthermore, his articles began appearing in such magazines as *Century, Harper's, The American Mercury,* and the *Crisis.*[7]

---

3. James Weldon Johnson, *The Book of American Negro Poetry,* p. 114.
4. James Weldon Johnson, *Along This Way,* New York, Viking, 1934.
5. James Weldon Johnson, *Black Manhattan,* New York, Knopf, 1930. [The book was reprinted in 1991 by Da Capro Press with an introduction by Sondra Kathryn Wilson.]
6. Countee Cullen, *Caroling Dusk,* p. 16.
7. Stanley J. Kunitz, *op. cit.,* p. 198.

The occasional work that James Weldon Johnson has done to enlighten the American public in regard to Negro literature and art and the encouragement that he has given young writers by opening new avenues of expression cannot be easily overestimated; and as lawyer, poet, musical composer, diplomatic official, editor, orator, critic, historian, and educator he has gazed on wider horizons than most of his fellows.[8]

For fourteen years he served as field secretary and then as secretary for the National Association for the Advancement of Colored People. It was his able statement of the case against lynching that finally brought the great agitation of the pros and cons of the proposed Dyer Anti-Lynching Bill.

His investigations of conditions in Haiti during the American Occupation called the attention of the public and the Congress to marine misrule in the island. His subsequent articles in the *Nation* created something of a furor; and Senator Harding took up the issues, as a result of which a Naval Board of Inquiry was sent to Haiti and a little later an Educational Board, including representatives from Howard University and Tuskegee Institute.

Talladega College and Howard University have conferred on him the degree of Litt. D. He is a director of the American Fund of Public Service, a member of the Ethical Society of American, the Academy of Political Science, and a trustee of Atlanta University.[9] He received the Spingarn Medal in 1925 for distinguished service. He has lectured on literary subjects at many colleges and universities, and at present divides his time between Fisk University and New York University.

The Critic

In his *Book of American Negro Poetry*[10] Mr. Johnson's taste as a critic is revealed in two ways: first, in the introductory essay on creative Negro genius, which initiated work in a new field, Mr. Johnson made certain predictions that recent facts have verified; and, second, his fine literary judg-

8. Robert T. Kerlin, *Negro Poets and Their Poems,* pp. 90–91.
9. Stanley J. Kunitz, *op. cit.,* p. 198.
10. James Weldon Johnson, *The Book of American Negro Poetry,* New York, Harcourt & Brace, 1922. [The book was revised in 1931 under the auspices of the Julius Rosenwald Fund. Tolson consistently cites this edition.]

ments were exercised in the selections and interpretations of the illustrative materials.

Mr. William Rose Benét, who with Henry Seidel Canby and Christopher Morley, started the *Saturday Review of Literature,* was impressed by the book to this degree:

> No single volume so deeply discloses the soul of the Negro. . . . Mr. Johnson has made his selections with the taste of the poet and the thorough knowledge of the extant poetry of his race.[11]

A Mulatto Passes

The Autobiography of an Ex-Colored Man was a book that took up the old, old question of "passing," which has intrigued many writers of novels and dramas. Perhaps Johnson's story is nearer the truth than most stories of this type, in that his mulatto pianist does not experience those sentimental yearnings to return to his people as portrayed in the works of writers who straddle the fence of convention, with one eye cocked on the weather vane of public opinion. A London critic saw in the book a soul-revelation as microscopically clear as that discovered in Booker T. Washington's widely read autobiography: "Nothing more revealing of the mind of the Negro has been published since *Up from Slavery.*"[12]

God's Trombones[13]

James Weldon Johnson's reputation as a poet will probably rest securely in American Literature on that unique volume *God's Trombones.* In that book he reproduced the sermons of the old Negro preacher who is fast fading from the scene. The words are the words of these trombones of God.

11. William Rose Benét, "American Negro Poetry," *Saturday Review of Literature,* Vol. 7, p. 714 (April 4, 1931).
12. *London Spectator,* Vol. 140, p. 267 (February 25, 1928).
13. James Weldon Johnson, *God's Trombones,* New York, Viking, 1927.

The title in itself is significant. The trombone is an instrument, blaring, regal, triumphant. It's place in the Negro band is uncontested. The other instruments do obeisance to it, and the player of the trombone is aware of this. He has a dignity that struts. Now, the old Negro preacher looked upon himself as the instrument of God. He was not concerned with quibbles about evolution and homiletic antimonies. He moved about the pulpit in majesty and glory and blatancy.

A writer in the *Saturday Review of Literature* made the following generalization:

> No one who wishes to familiarize himself with the most artistic and native work that is coming from the literate Negroes of today can afford to neglect this slim, beautiful volume of Mr. Johnson's.[14]

Mr. Johnson took a divergent angle in recording the sermons of these ante-bellum mouthpieces of Christianity as black men understood it. Arthur Guiterman, himself deeply interested in historical and legendary ballads, comments on the fact that Mr. Johnson, in contrast with Dunbar's use of dialect for his Negro sermons, fails to follow in the footsteps of his forerunner:

> Mr. Johnson's good taste has rejected dialect and low comedy, and his interpretations are genuinely and deeply moving.[15]

Countee Cullen in his novel *One Way to Heaven*[16] revealed his intimate knowledge of these humbler members of the religious order, and thus his word is invaluable in authenticating Mr. Johnson's observations and delineations of these trombones of God:

> The poet here has admirably risen to his intentions and his needs; entombed in this bright mausoleum the Negro preacher of an older day

---

14. *Saturday Review of Literature,* Vol. 3, p. 904, (June 2, 1927).
15. Arthur Guiterman, ["Poems Opaque, Translucent, and Clear,"] *Outlook,* Vol. 141, p. 319 (July 6, 1927).
16. Countee Cullen, *One Way to Heaven,* New York, Harper, 1932.

> can never pass entirely deathward . . . This verse is simple and awful at once, the grand diapason of a musician playing on an organ with far more than two keys.[17]

Along This Way

In 1933 James Weldon Johnson paused to collect the experiences of a life that had touched many phases of human existence, and the result was *Along This Way,*[18] which, when Miss Harriet Monroe had read her autographed copy in the office of *Poetry: A Magazine of Verse,* led this friend of poets to say: "Here is one of the great books of our time."[19]

Ms. Monroe had been a quiet but faithful supporter of the Harlem poets, encouraging them, and publishing many of their poems in her journal, along with the experimental works of Vachal Lindsay, Carl Sandburg, Rabindranath Tagore, Robert Frost, Rupert Brooks, and others.[20]

Along This Way was a full-bodied narrative of the social, political, and cultural adventures of a strikingly unusual personality.[21] There was a felicitous blend of the material and the style of the story teller. It was civilized in temper, ironical, urbane, deft, and reflective, and this led Mr. Gallard to call it "the most cleverly written indictment of the American caste system which has come to hand."[22] Johnson's stylistic competence inspired Mr. E. R. Embree of the Rosenwald Foundation to consider the "English so good that one forgets to notice how well it is written."[23]

---

17. Countee Cullen, ["And the Walls Came Tumblin' Down,"] *Bookman,* Vol. 66, p. 221 (October, 1927).
18. James Weldon Johnson, *Along This Way,* New York, Viking, 1934.
19. Footnote: Quotation taken from an interview with Miss Harriet Monroe in the spring of 1934.
20. Harriet Monroe and A. C. Henderson, *The New Poetry, An Anthology* (rev. and enl.), New York, 1932.
21. Zona Gale, "Johnson's Autobiography," *World Tomorrow,* Vol. 17, p. 20 (January 4, 1934).
22. J. T. Gallard, ["Autobiography of the New Negro,"] *Commonweal,* Vol. 19, p. 82 (November 17, 1933).
23. E. R. Embree, "Along This Way," *Survey,* Vol. 22, p. 568 (November 1933).

If this most versatile of Negroes does nothing additional to lend lustre to his name, what he has already accomplished will assure him of a place in the literature of the country whose ideals he has so earnestly tried to translate in terms of reality.[24]

24. Mary White Ovington, "James Weldon Johnson," *Portraits in Color,* pp. 1–17.

Chapter 13

Wallace Thurman

His Life

Wallace Thurman, critic, novelist, and editor, was born in Salt Lake City, Utah, in 1902.[1] He knew every member of the Harlem group intimately, because he was the editor-in-chief of the two magazines which the group published in the heyday of the Harlem Renaissance.[2] Because of his enthusiastic work among the younger members, Wallace Thurman, whose cynicism finally led him to denounce the Renaissance as a fad, in that earlier period became known as "the oracle of the New Negro."[3]

He was educated in the public schools of Boise, Idaho, and of Salt Lake City. He finished high school in three years, spent two years in the University of Utah and completed his formal education in the University of California.[4]

While working at the post office in Los Angeles, Thurman and two other mail carriers started a monthly magazine, and as editor he announced the policy of the publication in the following exuberant language of youth:

1. V. F. Calverton, *Anthology of American Negro Literature,* p. 534. [For a good overview of his work see Eleonore Van Notten, *Wallace Thurman's Harlem Renaissance.*]
2. Wallace Thurman, *Fire,* Vol. 1, p. 47 (November 1926).
3. *Crisis,* Vol. 34, p. 12 (May 1927).
4. V. F. Calverton, *op. cit.,* p. 534.

> *The Outlet* will seek each month to discover and propagate the best that is known and thought by Negroes in the World of Literature. It will be the incubator of Genius.[5]

Thurman remarked in an interview that the main purpose of the magazine was to serve as an outlet for the editor's own stories and essays.[6] Attending college, working at the post office, and editing a magazine could lead to nothing but failure in one or more of the attempts. Thurman was concerned with the literary side of the venture, and so the project collapsed financially; but the editorial training secured helped Thurman considerably when a little later he came to New York City.

Fire[7]

With the publication of *Fire,* a quarterly devoted to the younger Negro artists and writers, a milestone was reached in the Harlem Renaissance. Copies of this magazine have already become the items of bibliophiles because of the fire at 314 West 138th Street, where Mr. Thurman made his home until his death on December 21, 1934.[8]

Mr. Thurman says that the first meeting of the group that sponsored *Fire* was held in a cellar cafe in Greenwich Village.[9] Exhilarated by the wine supplied by a fortunate member, the proposition took on the character of a heroic venture and the financial aspect shriveled into the background. Here was a chance for the younger members of the Harlem group to declare their independence—of what or whom, the records do not show.

---

5. *The Outlet,* Vol. 1, p. 3 (December 1924).
6. Footnote: Interview with Mr. Thurman.
7. *Fire,* Vol. 1, p. 1 (November 1926). [For a good discussion of *Fire* see David Levering Lewis, *When Harlem Was in Vogue,* 194–97. Also see Rampersad, *The Life of Langston Hughes, Vol. I,* 134–38, 154 and 184.]
8. *Kansas City Call,* Vol. 16, p. 6 (January 4, 1935).
9. Footnote: Unprinted material supplied by Mr. Thurman in the spring of 1922, while serving as one of the editors of the Macaulay Publishing Company of New York.

Each member of the staff promised to advance $100.00. Langston Hughes, the poet, was the only one who was able to do this.

Wallace Thurman borrowed $150.00 from the loan department of the Harlem Community Church and a similar amount from the Mutual League. Professor Alain Locke, a fatherly bachelor in the Department of Philosophy at Howard University, pledged himself to take care of the remainder of the note.

Foreword of Fire[10]

Fire . . . flaming, burning, searing, and penetrating far beneath the superficial items of the flesh to boil the sluggish blood.

Fire . . . a cry of conquest in the night, warning those who sleep and revitalizing those who linger in the quiet places dozing.

Fire . . . melting steel and iron bars, poking livid tongues between the stone apertures and burning wooden opposition with a cackling chuckle of contempt.

Fire . . . weaving vivid, hot designs upon an ebony bordered loom and satisfying pagan thirst for beauty unadorned . . . flesh is sweet and real . . . the soul an inward flush of fire.— . . . beauty? . . . flesh on fire—on fire in the furnace of life blazing. . . .

Because of its historical value and the extreme rarity of copies of *Fire*, perhaps it will not be amiss to include in this essay the names of those who were associated with Mr. Thurman or who contributed to the first issue of the magazine:

Table of Contents[11]

10. "Foreward," *Fire*, Vol. 1, p. 2 (November 1926). [*Fire* was reprinted in 1982. See note 14 on p. 46.]
11. "Table of Contents," *Fire*, Vol. 1, p. 3 (November 1926).

On November 2, 1926, Langston Hughes wrote a letter to Wallace Thurman—a letter which is self-explanatory in it revelation of the financial incapacities of the various members of the editorial staff:

> Dear Wallie:
>
> Your "Foreword" is great, and I don't doubt but that the editorials will be fine, too. . . . Leave everybody's name on the list as editors whether they give anything or not. To drop them off on the next issue would look better than if they were omitted now, and would be more effective. Then we can take on fresh editors and blaze anew. Your ability as editor, advertising man, and all is marvelous. . . . Couldn't the versatile Zora borrow a few bucks for us? I couldn't possibly get any more money than twenty-five together any time soon. I'm ruined as it is.
>
> Langston[12]
>
> P.S. Get $10 from Aaron.

On November 9, 1926, Miss Gwendolyn Bennett, who was teaching at the time in the Department of Fine Arts, at Howard University, wrote to Wallace Thurman:

12. Footnote: Copied from the original letter in the possession of Mr. Thurman. It is believed that the letters were lost in the fire.

Dear Wallie:

I feel like a bum not to have been able to send you a cent before this, but you will understand I'm sure, when you realize that I am my mother's sole support. It seems that it has taken every penny that I could earn, beg, borrow, or steal to keep things going. But when you realize that I shall have to do without a winter coat for a few more months, you know that my heart is in the right place anyway.

Gwendolyn[13]

Then to add to the grim misfortunes of the group one night as Thurman was walking down a Harlem street with most of the money for the publication in his pocket, he was held up and most of his clothes and all of the money were taken from him. The editor of *Fire* had to borrow a suit to attend to his executive duties the next day! Thurman sent a telegram to Langston Hughes, who was in attendance at Lincoln University in Pennsylvania, inquiring if the poet had any plan by which the oracle of the Harlem Renaissance could be brought before the public. Hughes replied in his characteristic vein:

Dear Wallie:

Sorry as I can be about the loss. Here is a buck to help you on carfare anyway. Leaves me with thirty-six cents. May have $25 for *Fire* next week. Just now I'm lowdown. But we'll come through somehow, I'm sure. Trust in God! (I'm feeling very religious now!) Fy-ah's gonna burn ma soul!

Langston[14]

And this was the letter of encouragement, shot through with poetic faith, which the poor editor-in-chief received from his most famous colleague. In spite of all difficulties, *Fire* came out in a blaze of glory that thrilled at least the editorial staff. The editor received the following letter from Irita Van Doren:

Dear Mr. Thurman:

I read the first copy of *Fire* with much interest and was glad to use it more or less as a text for an informal talk at the National Art Club the

13. Footnote: Quoted from the original letter in Mr. Thurman's possession.
14. Footnote: Quoted from Mr. Hughes' letter to Mr. Thurman.

other night. It is just the sort of magazine I had hoped for some time young Negro writers would produce, and I wish you all success.

Irita Van Doren[15]

Carl Van Vechten, who had done a great deal to popularize Negro art and literature, before his *Nigger Heaven* caused him to lose his prestige in Harlem, wrote to the editor as follows:

Dear Wallace Thurman:

Put this in your *fire* and burn it! Yours for a blaze.

Carl Van Vechten[16]

February 15, 1926.

On December 3, 1926, Mr. George Jean Nathan, an eminent critic of the American stage, gave his impressions of the magazine in a single sentence:

My dear Mr. Thurman:

I have read *Fire* from cover to cover and have found it a thoroughly interesting magazine.

Sincerely yours,

George Jean Nathan[17]

Professor Alain Locke in his review compared *Fire* with three other little magazines that were seeking to foster artistic talent in America at the time:

The bold, arresting red and black jacket is not accidental: the *Little Review, This Quarter,* and *The Quill* are obvious artistic cousins.[18]

15. Footnote: From the letters in Mr. Thurman's collection.
16. Footnote: *Ibid.* [See Nathan Huggins, *Harlem Renaissance,* 191–95, for a good discussion of Thurman's novels.]
17. Footnote: *Ibid.*
18. Alain Locke, "Fire," *Survey Graphic,* Vol. 53, p. 631 (March 1, 1927). [The title, based on volume and page number, is "Enter the New Negro." There is no reference to *Fire.*]

Out in the Middle West, an editorial in the *Minnesota Student* found the poems and stories and drawings "vivid and challenging."[19]

On the other hand, Mr. Reas Graves was disgusted with the magazine, in that most of the stories portrayed the lower levels of Harlem life, phases that reflect on the better class of Negroes; therefore, he felt justified in doing the following:

> I have just tossed the first issue of *Fire,* the new magazine devoted to and by the younger Negro artists, into the fire and watched the cackling flames leap and snarl as though they were trying to swallow some repulsive dose.[20]

Harlem

In November 1928, *Harlem,* a forum of Negro life, was brought out by the younger group of writers. It did not create the stir that its forerunner *Fire*[21] had created, but it is important historically because it gave the younger group an opportunity for self-expression, and the contents of the organ revealed the fact that several of the contributors who later became well known had already determined the milieu they would exploit artistically and the style they would use in their art and poems and novels. Wallace Thurman was again the editor-in-chief.

Some of the leading contributors to *Harlem* were Walter White, Langston Hughes, Alain Locke, George Schuyler, Wallace Thurman, Aaron Douglas, the mural painter, Theophilus Lewis, the critic of drama, Alice Dunbar-Nelson, the short story writer, and Helene Johnson, the poet.[22]

The Novelist

Wallace Thurman established himself as a novelist with the publication of *The Blacker the Berry,*[23] containing a theme which struck right at the roots

19. *Minnesota Student,* Vol. 12, p. 4 (January 1, 1927).
20. Rean Graves, *Baltimore Afro-American,* Vol. XX, p. 8 (December 10, 1926).
21. Footnote: *Fire* ran only two issues and *Harlem* three.
22. "Table of Contents," *Harlem,* Vol. 1, p. 3 (November 1928).
23. Wallace Thurman, *The Blacker the Berry,* New York, Macaulay, 1929.

of a peculiar type of prejudice, a realistic study of the color lines within the color line.

The story of Emma Lou, a dark-skinned educated woman, a social outcast among her own people because they prefer women of a lighter hue, is a thing that twists the heartstrings. Mr. Thurman keeps her in settings which will emphasize the irony and pathos of her character. The *Bookman* was more impressed with the novel because of its explorations into the bypaths of Negro psychology than with its "sordid, rather heavily written" style.[24] Professor Alain Locke, like most of the other critics, was fascinated by the tragedy of the theme, but in regard to the craftsmanship of Wallace Thurman he was forced to this conclusion:

> Mr. Thurman's first novel must be regarded as a ground-breaker only, as calling attention to an important theme—Emma Lou, the dark girl's story, must be written sometime with greater art and a truer sense of values.[25]

In 1932 Wallace Thurman brought out *Infants of the Spring,*[26] which was a novel dealing in a realistic way with the poets and novelists and artists with whom Thurman was associated in the Harlem Renaissance, and many of the figures that move through the pages of the book can be readily recognized, to the extent that one woman threatened to bring suit against the author; nevertheless, some critics have asserted that his characters are ciphers. Thurman, unflinchingly honest, put himself in the book.

Thurman alienated the affection of many of his early associates, as the years turned him into a profound cynic. As the "oracle of the Renaissance," he proclaimed it a worthless fad and considered his own work trashy. He drank heavily and delighted in castigating his contemporaries. However, one cannot doubt that, in spite of Thurman's well-advertised sophistication and his wisecracking propensity, even when dealing with

---

24. *Bookman,* Vol. 69, p. 24 (April 1929).
25. Alain Locke, ["Both Sides of the Color Line,"] *Survey,* Vol. 62, p. 325 (June 1929).
26. Footnote: Opinions expressed by Mr. Thurman during several interviews.

serious subject matter, he feels with great acuteness; and one critic who reviewed *Infants of the Spring* considers him "the most truthful Negro writer in America today."[27]

27. Martha Gruening, ["Two Ways to Harlem,"] *Saturday Review of Literature*, Vol. 8, p. 585 (March 12, 1932).

In Conclusion

The Harlem Renaissance came with startling immediacy, and Negro America grew conscious of the inflowing of a powerful verve. The exuberant Paul Robeson and the gentle-mannered Roland Hayes gave their individual interpretations of the spirituals in concert halls. Negro historians like W.E.B. Du Bois, Arthur Schomburg, Carter G. Woodson, and Charles S. Johnson made explorations into the cultural backgrounds of the Negro and African peoples. Magazines like *The Crisis, Opportunity, Fire,* and *Harlem* encouraged the younger writers and artists. Critics of sound scholarship, like Alain Locke, James Weldon Johnson, and William Stanley Braithwaite interpreted the movement for a growing white public. The literature that came out of the Harlem Renaissance, which has been the focal point of this thesis, affected and was affected by the larger culture of the new literature that began with the publication of the first issue of *Poetry* by Harriet Monroe in 1912.

Many thought that the Harlem Renaissance was just a fad. In this they were mistaken. It has been followed by a proletarian literature of Negro life, wider in scope, deeper in significance, and better in stylistic methods. Perhaps an editorial in *New Challenge,* edited by members of the new school, gives us the best summary of the old and the new in Negro literature:

> We are not attempting to restage the "revolt" and "renaissance" which grew unsteadily and upon false foundations ten years ago. A literary movement among Negroes, we feel, should, first of all, be built upon the writer's placing his material in the proper perspective with regard to the Negro masses. For that reason we want to indicate, through examples in our pages, the fertility of folk material as a source of creative material. . . .

> We hope that through our pages we may be able to point social directives and provide a basis for the clear recognition of and solution to the problems which face the contemporary writer.[1]

One who is familiar with the new school of Negro writers—Zora Hurston, Edward Turpin, Marshall Davis, George Lee, O'Wendell Shaw, and Richard Wright—is impressed with the radical change in point of view. Most of the members of the Harlem Renaissance portrayed the sensational features of Negro life, which were exploited for the entertainment of white readers. The literature of today is earthy, unromantic, and sociological; and from it emerges Negro characters that are more graphically individualized.

1. "Editorial," *New Challenge,* Vol. 11, p. 3 (Fall 1937).

Bibliography

General

American Caravan, The, New York, Macaulay, 1927.

Blankenship, Russell, *American Literature,* New York, Henry Holt, 1931, pp. 43–45, pp. 639–648.

Braithwaite, William Stanley, "The Negro in American Literature," in *The New Negro,* edited by Alain Locke, Albert & Charles Boni, New York, 1925, p. 29.

Bechhofer, C. E., *The Literary Renaissance in America,* London, Heinnemann, 1923.

Brawley, Benjamin, *The Negro in Literature and Art,* New York, Duffield, 1926.

A Short History of the American Negro, New York, Macmillan, 1919.

A Social History of the American Negro, New York, Macmillan, 1921.

Calverton, V. F., *Anthology of American Negro Literature,* New York, Modern Library, 1929.

Carter, Elmer A., *Opportunity,* Vol. 10, p. 85 (March 1932).

Chamberlain, J., "Negro as Writer," *Bookman,* Vol. 70, p. 603 (February 1930).

Crowell, J. W., *The Negro in American History,* Washington, D.C., American Negro Academy, 1914.

Cullen, Countee, *Caroling Dusk,* New York, Harper, 1927.

Culp, D. W., *Twentieth Century Negro Literature,* Naperville, Illinois, Nichols, 1902.

Detweiler, Frederick G., *The Negro Press in the United States,* Chicago, University of Chicago Press, 1923.

Dowd, Jerome, *The Negro in American Life,* New York, Century, 1926.

Du Bois, W. E. B., *The Gift of Black Folk,* Boston, Stratford, 1924.

Fisher, Rudolph, "The Caucasian Storms Harlem," *American Mercury,* Vol. 2, pp. 393–398 (August 1927).

Galton, Francis, *Hereditary Genius, An Inquiry into Its Laws and Consequences,* London, 1869.

"Harlem," *Encyclopaedia Britannica,* fourteenth edition,Vol. 16, p. 200.

Hartt, R. L., "I'd Like to Show You Harlem," *Independent,* Vol. 105, p. 334 (April 2, 1921).

Johnson, Charles S., *Ebony and Topaz,* New York, Opportunity, 1927.

Johnson, James Weldon, "Race Prejudice and the Negro Artist," *Harper,* Vol. 157, p. 771 (November 1928).

The Book of American Negro Poetry, Harcourt & Brace, New York, 1931.

Journal of Negro History, edited by Carter G. Woodson, Washington, Associated Press, 1911.

Kerlin, Robert J., *Negro Poets and Their Poems,* Washington, Associated Press, 1923.

The Voice of the Negro, New York, Dutton, 1920.

King, Willis J., *The Negro in American Life,* Chicago, Methodist Book Concern, 1926.

Lewishon, Ludwig, *The Creative Life,* New York, Boni & Liveright, 1924, p. 17.

Locke, Alain, *Four Negro Poets,* New York, Simon & Schuster, 1927.

The New Negro, New York, Albert & Charles Boni, 1925.

Morton, Beatrice, *Negro Poetry in America,* Boston, Stratford, 1925.

"Negro Artists and the Negro," *New Republic,* Vol. 52, pp. 37–39 (August 1927).

"Negro City," *Review of Reviews,* Vol. 73, p. 323 (March 1926).

Negro Year Book, edited yearly by Professor Monroe N. Work, Tuskegee Institute, Tuskegee, Alabama.

O'Brien, Edward J., *The Advance of the American Short Story,* New York, Dodd & Mead, 1923.

The Best Short Stories of 1925, New York, Small & Maynard, 1925.

Odum, H. W., *Saturday Review of Literature,* Vol. 6, p. 2 (July 27, 1929).

Ovington, Mary White, *Portraits in Color,* New York, Viking, 1927.

Pattee, Fred Lewis, *The Development of the American Short Story,* New York, Century, 1927, p. 238.

Rose, E., "Serving New York's Black City," *Library Journal,* Vol. 48.

Scribling, T. J., "The Real Harlem," *New York World,* March 11, 1928.

Slater, John R., *Rhetoric,* New York, Heath, 1913, pp. 291–299.

Smith, S. Stephenson, *The Craft of the Critic,* New York, Crowell, 1931, pp. 14–28.

Sanborn, Gertrude, *Veiled Aristocrats,* Washington, Associated Press, 1924.

Untermeyer, Louis, *American Poetry Since 1900,* New York, Holt, 1923.

Van Doren, Carl, "Negro Renaissance," *Century,* Vol. 3, pp. 635–637.

Van Vechten, Carl, *Nigger Heaven,* New York, Knopf, 1926, p. 15.

Warner, Arthur, "The Negro World's Capital," New York, *Dunbar News,* October 8, 1930.

Harlem and the Forces in the Harlem Renaissance

Blankenship, Russell, *American Literature*, New York, Holt, 1931, p. 244.

Calverton, V. F., *Anthology of American Negro Literature*, New York, Modern Library, 1929, p. 13.

Carter, Elmer, "Harlem," *Opportunity*, Vol. 10, p. 85 (March 1932).

Chamberlain, J., "Negro As Writer," *Bookman*, Vol. 70, pp. 603–611 (February 1930).

Fisher, Rudolph, "The Caucasian Storms Harlem," *American Mercury*, Vol. 11, pp. 393–398 (August 1927).

Fire, Vol. 1, p. 2 (November 1926).

Herskovits, Melville, *The American Negro*, New York, Knopf, 1928, p. 17.

Johnson, James Weldon, "Race Prejudice and the Negro Artist," *Harper*, Vol. 157, p. 771 (November 1928).

Kerlin, Robert Thomas, *Negro Poets and Their Poems*, Washington, Associated Press, 1923, p. 1.

Locke, Alain, *The New Negro*, New York, Albert & Charles Boni, 1925, p. 7.

Nearing, Scott, *Black America*, New York, Viking, 1929, p. 122.

Stribling, T. J., "The Real Harlem," *New York World*, March 11, 1928.

Thurman, Wallace, *Harlem*, Vol. 1, p. 31 (November 1928).

Van Vechten, Carl, *Nigger Heaven*, New York, Knopf, 1926.

Van Doren, Carl, "Negro Renaissance," *Century*, Vol. 111, pp. 635–637 (March 1926).

White, Walter, "The Negro Mecca," *New York World Telegram*, December 25, 1931.

Countee Cullen

Published Works

Caroling Dusk, New York, Harper, 1927.

Color, New York, Harper, 1925.

Copper Sun, New York, Harper, 1927.

One Way to Heaven, New York, Harper, 1932.

The Ballad of the Brown Girl, New York, Harper, 1927.

The Black Christ and Other Poems, New York, Harper, 1929.

Criticisms

Blankenship, Russell, *American Literature*, New York, Holt, 1931, p. 645.

Bookman, Vol. 62, p. 503 (December, 1925).
Gorman, Herbert, "Countee Cullen," *Nation,* Vol. 125, p. 518 (November 9, 1927).
Independent, Vol. 115, p. 539 (November 1925).
Johnson, James Weldon, *The Book of American Negro Poetry,* p. 220.
Kreymborg, Alfred, *Our Singing Strength,* New York, Cowan & McCann, 1929, p. 576.
Kunitz, Stanley, *Living Authors,* New York, Wilson, 1931, p. 89.
Literary Digest, Vol. 115, p. 5 (November 1925).
Poetry, Vol. 28, pp. 50–53 (April 1926).
Survey, Vol. 53, pp. 660–1 (March 1, 1925).
Survey, Vol. 59, p. 184 (November 1, 1927).
World Tomorrow, Vol. 10, p. 472 (November 1927).

Langston Hughes

Published Works

Dramatic Recitations, New York, Golden Star Publishers, 1932.
Fine Clothes to the Jew, New York, Knopf, 1927.
Not Without Laughter, New York, Knopf, 1930.
The Ways of White Folks, New York, Knopf, 1934.
The Weary Blues, New York, Knopf, 1926.

Criticisms

Anderson, Sherwood, "Langston Hughes," *Nation,* Vol. 139, p. 49 (July 11, 1934).
Blankenship, Russell, *American Literature,* p. 642.
Briggs, "The Sound and the Fury," *Esquire,* Vol. 1, p. 17 (May 1934).
Cullen, Countee, *Caroling Dusk,* New York, Harper, 1927, p. 144.
Hatcher, Harlan, *Creating the Modern American Novel,* p. 151
Johnson, James Weldon, *The Book of American Negro Poetry,* p. 232.
Kreymborg, Alfred, *Our Singing Strength,* p. 576.
Kunitz, Stanley, *Living Authors,* p. 184.
Locke, Alain, "The Negro in American Culture," *Anthology of American Negro Literature,* edited by V. F. Calverton, New York, Modern Library, 1929, p. 256.
Monroe, Harriet, "Langston Hughes," *The New Poetry,* New York, Macmillan, 1932, p. 719.
Tolson, Melvin, "Goodbye Christ," *Pittsburgh Courier,* Vol. XXIII, pp. 10–11 (January 26, 1933).

Claude McKay

Published Works

Banjo, New York, Harper, 1929.
Banana Bottom, New York, Harper, 1933.
Gingertown, New York, Harper, 1932.
Harlem Shadows, New York, Harcourt & Brace, 1922.
Home to Harlem, New York, Harper, 1927.

Criticisms

Cullen, Countee, *Caroling Dusk,* p. 81.
Connolly, Cyril, "Novelist of Harlem," *New Statesman,* Vol. 31, p. 591 (August 18, 1928).
Hatcher, Harlan, *Creating the Modern American Novel,* p. 151.
Kirchwey, Freda, "Claude McKay," *Nation,* Vol. 128, p. 614 (May 22, 1929).
Kirnon, Hodge, "Claude McKay," *West Indian Review,* Vol. 1, p. 17 (January-February 1932).
Kunitz, Stanley, *Living Authors,* p. 243.
Mortimer, R., "The Jamaican," *Nation and Athenaeum,* Vol. 43, p. 397 (June 23, 1928).
Nation, Vol. 136, p. 564 (May 17, 1933).
Odum, H. W., "Harlem," *Saturday Review of Literature,* Vol. 6, p. 2 (July 27, 1929).
Outlook, Vol. 148, p. 636 (April 18, 1928).
Rascoe, Burton, ["The Seamy Side,"] *Bookman,* Vol. 67, p. 183 (April 1928).
Saturday Review of Literature, Vol. 9, p. 529 (April 8, 1933).
Van Doren, Mark, *Nation,* Vol. 126, p. 351 (March 28, 1928).
Whipple, Leon, "Return of a Soldier," *Survey,* Vol. 60, p. 178 (May 1, 1928).
White, Walter, ["Negro Poets,"] *Nation,* Vol. 114, p. 694 (June 7, 1922).
White, Walter, ["The Negro Contribution,"] *Bookman,* Vol. 55, p. 531 (June 1922).

Walter White

Published Works

Flight, New York, Knopf, 1926.
Rope and Faggott, New York, Knopf, 1929.
The Fire in the Flint, New York, Knopf, 1924.

Criticisms

Bercovici, Konrad, ["Almost White and Black,"] *Nation,* Vol. 119, p. 389 (October 8, 1924).

Bookman, Vol. 60, p. 342 (November 1924).
Brichell, Herchel, *Literary Review,* November 1, 1924.
Calverton, V. F., *Anthology of American Negro Literature,* p. 535.
Crawford, J. W., "Flight," *Independent,* Vol. 116, p. 519 (June 1, 1926).
Faris, Ellsworth, ["The Cave Man Within Us,"] *New Republic,* Vol. 58, p. 338 (May 1929).
Independent, Vol. 116, p. 519 (June 1, 1926).
Green, Elizabeth Lay, *The Negro in Contemporary American Literature,* p. 44.
Ovington, Mary White, *Portraits in Color,* New York, Viking Press, 1927, p. 110.
Panghorn, H. L., "Fire in the Flint," *Independent,* Vol. 115, p. 850 (November 1924).
Saturday Review of Literature, Vol. 2, p. 918 (June 10, 1926).

Eric Walrond

Published Works

Big Ditch, New York, Boni & Liveright, 1928.
Tropic Death, New York, Boni & Liveright, 1926.

Criticisms

Calverton, V. F., ["Ground Swells in Fiction,"] *Survey,* Vol. 57, p. 160 (November 1, 1926).
Green, Elizabeth Lay, *The Negro in Contemporary American Literature,* p. 534.
Herrick, Robert, ["Tropic Death,"] *New Republic,* Vol. 48, p. 332 (November 10, 1926).
Independent, Vol. 117, pp. 260–262 (January, 1926).
Rosenfeld, Paul, *Men Seen,* New York, Dial Press, 1925, p. 232.

Rudolph Fisher

Published Works

The Conjure-Man Dies, New York, Covici, 1932.
The Walls of Jericho, New York, Knopf, 1928.

Criticisms

Best Short Stories of 1925, edited by Edward O'Brien, New York, Small & Maynard, 1925.

Readings from Negro Authors, edited by Cromwell, Turner, and Dykes, Harcourt & Brace, 1931.
Saturday Review of Literature, Vol. 5, p. 110 (September 8, 1928).
Saturday Review of Literature, Vol. 146, p. 250 (August 25, 1928).
London Spectator, Vol. 141, p. 252 (August 25, 1928).
Van Vechten, Carl, *Nigger Heaven,* New York, Knopf, 1926, pp. 255–260.
Weber, W. C., "The Walls of Jericho," *Saturday Review of Literature,* Vol. 9, p. 47 (August 13, 1932).

Jessie Fauset

Published Works

Chinaberry Tree, New York, Stokes, 1932.
Comedy: American Style, New York, Stokes, 1933.
Plum Bun, New York, Stokes, 1929.
There is Confusion, New York, Boni & Liveright, 1924.

Criticisms

Calverton, V. F., *Anthology of American Negro Literature,* p. 534.
Cullen, Countee, *Caroling Dusk,* p. 65.
Hatcher, Harlan, *Creating the Modern American Novel,* p. 151.
Independent Book Review, Vol. 13, p. 48 (June 24, 1924).
Johnson, James Weldon, *The Book of American Negro Poetry,* p. 205.
Nation, Vol. 138, p. 26 (January 3, 1934).
Nation, Vol. 135, p. 88 (July 27, 1932).
New Republic, Vol. 39, p. 192 (July 9, 1924).

George Schuyler

Published Works

Black No More, New York, Macaulay, 1931.
Slaves Today, New York, Harcourt & Brace, 1932.

Criticisms

America's News, Vol. 8, p. 10 (August 20, 1927).
Baltimore Afro-American, Vol. 25, p. 16 (December 3, 1927).
Bookman, Vol. 72, p. 8 (February 1931).

Calverton, V. F., *Anthology of American Negro Literature,* New York, Modern Library, 1929, p. 534.
Hatcher, Harlan, *op. cit,* p. 255.
Nation, Vol. 132, p. 218 (February 28, 1931).
Negro World, New York, Vol. 5, p. 8 (September 3, 1927).
Saturday Review of Literature, Vol. 7, p. 799 (May 2, 1931).
Survey, Vol. 66, p. 290 (June 1, 1931).
Van Doren, Dorothy, "George Schuyler," *Nation,* Vol. 132, p. 218 (February 25, 1931).

William Edward Burghardt Du Bois

Published Works

Black Reconstruction, New York, Harcourt & Brace, 1935.
Dark Water, New York, Harcourt & Brace, 1920.
John Brown, Philadelphia, Jacobs, 1909.
The Dark Princess, New York, Harcourt & Brace, 1928.
The Gift of Black Folk, Boston, Stratford, 1924.
The Negro, New York, Holt, 1915.
The Negro in the South, Philadelphia, Jacobs, 1907.
The Quest of the Silver Fleece, Chicago, McClurg, 1911.
The Souls of Black Folk, Chicago, McClurg, 1903.
The Star of Ethiopia: A Pageant, New York, The Horizon Guild, 1913.
The Suppression of the African Slave Trade, Harvard University Press, 1896.

Criticisms

American Mercury, Vol. 3, pp. 179–185 (October 1924).
Atlantic Monthly, Vol. 115, pp. 707–714 (May 1915).
Bookman, Vol. 60, p. 357 (November 1924).
Calvin, Floyd, *Pittsburgh Courier,* Vol. 25, p. 24, July 6, 1935.
Forum, Vol. 73, pp. 178–188 (February 1925).
Independent, Vol. 102, p. 235 (May 15, 1920).
Johnson, James Weldon, *The Book of American Negro Poetry,* p. 89.
Locke, Alain, *The New Negro,* New York, Albert & Charles Boni, p. 419.
Miller, Kelly, "The Crisis Magazine," *New York Amsterdam News,* April 13, 1932.
New Republic, Vol. 37, pp. 142–145 (January 2, 1924).

Ovington, Mary White, "W. E. B. Du Bois," *Survey,* Vol. 59, p. 164 (November 1, 1924).
Reitell, Jane, "W. E. B. Du Bois," *Annals American Academy,* Vol. 140, p. 347 (November 1928).
Woodson, Carter, *The Negro in Our History,* Washington, Associated Publishers, 1922, p. 487.
World Tomorrow, Vol. 11, p. 473 (November 1928).

James Weldon Johnson

Published Works

Along This Way, New York, Viking, 1934.
Autobiography of an Ex-Colored Man, New York, Sherman & French, 1912.
Black Manhattan, New York, Knopf, 1930.
The Book of American Negro Poetry, New York, Harcourt & Brace, 1922.
The Book of American Negro Spirituals, New York, Viking, 1925.
Fifty Years and Other Poems, New York, Viking, 1928.
God's Trombones, New York, Viking, 1927.
The Second Book of American Negro Spirituals, New York, Viking, 1926.

Criticisms

Benét, W. R., "American Negro Poetry," *Saturday Review of Literature,* Vol. 7, p. 714 (April 4, 1931).
Bookman, Vol. 66, p. 221 (October 1927).
Christian Century, Vol. 48, p. 716 (May 27, 1931).
Cullen, Countee, "Negro Poetry," *Bookman,* Vol. 66, p. 221 (October 1927).
Cullen, Countee, *Caroling Dusk,* p. 16.
Embree, E. R., "James Weldon Johnson," *Survey,* Vol. 22, p. 568 (November 1933).
Gale, Zona, "Along This Way," *World Tomorrow,* Vol. 17, p. 20 (January 4, 1934).
Gallard, J. T., ["Autobiography of the New Negro,"] *Commonweal,* Vol. 19, p. 82 (November 17, 1933).
Guiterman, Arthur, ["Poems Opaque, Translucent, and Clear" *Outlook,* Vol. 141, p. 320 (July 6, 1927).
Kerlin, Robert T., *Negro Poets and Their Poems,* p. 91.
Kunitz, Stanley, *Living Authors,* p. 197.
London Spectator, Vol. 140, p. 267 (February 25, 1928).

Ovington, Mary White, *Portraits in Color,* pp. 1–17.
Saturday Review of Literature, Vol. 3, p. 904 (June 2, 1927).

Wallace Thurman

Published Works

Harlem, an unpublished drama of Negro life.
Infants of the Spring, New York, Macaulay, 1932.
Interne, New York, Macaulay, 1932.
The Blacker the Berry, New York, Macaulay, 1929.

Criticisms

Calverton, V. F., *Anthology of American Negro Literature,* p. 534.
Crisis, Vol. 34, p. 12 (May 1927).
Fire, Vol. 1, p. 1 (November 1926).
Graves, Rean, "Wallace Thurman," *Baltimore Afro-American,* Vol. 20, p. 8 (December 10, 1926).
Gruening, Martha, ["Two Ways to Harlem,"] *Saturday Review of Literature,* Vol. 8, p. 585 (March 12, 1932).
Harlem, Vol. 1, p. 3 (November 1928).
Lewis, Theophilus, *New York Tattler,* Vol. 10, p. 38 (February 23, 1929).
Locke, Alain, *Survey,* Vol. 62, p. 325 (June 1929).
Nation, Vol. 134, p. 176 (February 10, 1932).
The Outlet, Vol. 1, p. 3 (December 1924).

Selected Bibliography

Melvin Tolson

Books

Bérubé, Michael. *Marginal Forces/ Cultural Centers: Tolson, Pynchon, and the Politics of the Canon.* Ithaca: Cornell UP, 1992.

Farnsworth, Robert M. *Melvin B. Tolson, 1898–1966: Plain Talk and Poetic Prophecy.* Columbia: U of Missouri P, 1984.

Flasch, Joy. *Melvin B. Tolson.* New York: Twayne Publishers, 1972.

Russell, Mariann. *Melvin B. Tolson's "Harlem Gallery": A Literary Analysis.* Columbia and London: U of Missouri P, 1980.

Editions

Farnsworth, Robert M., ed. *Caviar and Cabbage: Selected Columns by Melvin B. Tolson from the Washington Tribune, 1937–1944.* By Melvin Tolson. Columbia: U of Missouri P, 1982.

———, ed. *A Gallery of Harlem Portraits.* By Melvin Tolson. Columbia: U of Missouri P, 1979.

Nelson, Raymond, ed. *"Harlem Gallery" and Other Poems of Melvin Tolson.* Intro. Rita Dove. Charlottesville: UP of Virginia, 1999.

Dissertations

Bérubé, Michael Francis. "Marginal Forces/ Cultural Centers: Melvin Tolson, Thomas Pynchon, and the Rhetoric of Critical Response." U of Virginia, 1989.

Flasch, Joy. "Melvin B. Tolson: A Critical Biography." Oklahoma State U, 1969.

Huot, Robert J. "Melvin B. Tolson's 'Harlem Gallery': A Critical Edition with Introduction and Explanatory Notes." U of Utah, 1971.

Pinson, Hermine Dolorez. "The Aesthetic Evolution of Melvin B. Tolson: A Thematic Study of His Poetry." Rice U, 1991.

Williams, Wilburn. "The Desolate Servitude of Language: A Reading of the Poetry of Melvin B. Tolson." Yale U, 1979.

Woodson, Jon Stanton. "A Critical Analysis of the Poetry of Melvin B. Tolson." Brown U, 1978.

Articles

Anonymous. "A Poet's Odyssey." *Anger and Beyond: The Negro Writer in the United States.* Ed. Herbert Hill. New York: Harper & Row, 1966. 181–195.

Basler, Roy P. "The Heart of Blackness: M. B. Tolson's Poetry." *New Letters: A Magazine of Fine Writing* 39.3 (1973): 63–76.

Bérubé, Michael. "Avant-Gardes and De-Author-izations: Harlem Gallery and the Cultural Contradictions of Modernism." *Callaloo* 12.1 (1989): 192–215.

———. "Masks, Margins, and African American Modernism: Melvin Tolson's Harlem Gallery." *PMLA* 105.1 (1990): 57–69.

Cansler, Ronald L. "'The White and Non-White Dichotomy' of Melvin B. Tolson's Poetry." *Negro American Literature Forum* 7 (1973): 115–118.

Dove, Rita. "Telling It Like It I-S IS: Narrative Techniques in Melvin Tolson's Harlem Gallery." *New England Review & Bread Loaf Quarterly* 8.1 (1985): 109–117.

Farnsworth, Robert M. "Preface to Melvin B. Tolson's Caviar and Cabbage Columns." *New Letters: A Magazine of Fine Writing* 47.4 (1981): 101–102.

———. "What Can a Poet Do? Langston Hughes and M. B. Tolson." *New Letters: A Magazine of Fine Writing* 48.1 (1981): 19–29.

Flasch, Joy. "Humor and Satire in the Poetry of M. B. Tolson." *Satire Newsletter* 7 (1969): 29–36.

Hansell, William H. "Three Artists in Melvin B. Tolson's Harlem Gallery." *Black American Literature Forum* 18.3 (1984): 122–127.

Lenhart, Gary. "Caviar and Cabbage: The Voracious Appetite of Melvin Tolson." *American Poetry Review* 29.2 (2000): 35–40.

McCall, Dan. "The Quicksilver Sparrow of M. B. Tolson." *American Quarterly* 18 (1966): 538–542.

Mootry, Maria K. "'The Step of Iron Feet': Creative Practice in the War Sonnets of Melvin B. Tolson and Gwendolyn Brooks." *Obsidian II* 2.3 (1987): 69–87.

Nielsen, Aldon L. "Melvin B. Tolson and the Deterritorialization of Modernism." *African American Review* 26.2 (1992): 241–55.

Russell, Mariann B. "Evolution of Style in the Poetry of Melvin B. Tolson." *Black American Poets Between Worlds, 1940–1960.* Ed. R. Baxter Miller. Knoxville: U of Tennessee P, 1986. 1–18.

———. "Ghetto Laugher: A Note of Tolson's Style." *Obsidian: Black Literature in Review* 5.1–2 (1979): 7–16.

Schroeder, Patricia R. "Point and Counterpoint in Harlem Gallery." *CLA Journal* 27.2 (1983): 152–168.

Smith, Gary. "A Hamlet Rives Us: The Sonnets of Melvin B. Tolson." *CLA Journal* 29.3 (1986): 261–275.

Thompson, Gordon E. "Ambiguity in Tolson's Harlem Gallery." *Callaloo* 9.1 (1986): 159–70.

Tolson, Melvin B., Jr. "The Poetry of Melvin B. Tolson (1898–1966)." *World Literature Today: A Literary Quarterly of the University of Oklahoma* 64.3 (1990): 395–400.

Walcott, Ronald. "Some Notes on the Blues, Style & Space: Ellison, Gordone and Tolson." *Black World* 22.2 (1972): 4–29.

Wald, Alan. "Contradictions of the Canon." *Minnesota Review* 41–42 (1993–1994): 292–97.

Werner, Craig. "Blues for T. S. Eliot and Langston Hughes: Melvin Tolson: The Afro-Modernist Aesthetic of 'Harlem Gallery.'" *Black American Literature Forum* 24 (1990): 453–472.

Woodson, Jon. "Melvin and the Art of Being Difficult." *Black American Poets Between Worlds, 1940–1960.* Ed. R. Baxter Miller. Knoxville: U of Tennessee P, 1986. 19–42.

The Harlem Renaissance

Books

Abramson, Doris E. *Negro Playwrights in the American Theatre, 1925–1959.* New York: Columbia UP, 1969.

Adoff, Arnold. *I Am the Darker Brother: An Anthology of Modern Poems by Negro Americans.* New York: Macmillan, 1968.

Anderson, Jervis. *This Was Harlem: A Cultural Portrait, 1900–1950.* New York: Farrar, Straus & Giroux, 1982.

Andrews, William L. *Classic Fiction of the Harlem Renaissance.* New York: Oxford UP, 1994

Arata, Esther Spring. *More Black American Playwrights: A Bibliography.* Metuchen, NJ: Scarecrow, 1978.

Arata, Esther Spring, and Nicholas John Rotoli. *Black American Playwrights, 1800 to Present: A Bibliography.* Metuchen, NJ: Scarecrow, 1976.

Baker, Houston A., Jr. *Afro-American Poetics: Revisions of Harlem and the Black Aesthetic.* Madison: U of Wisconsin P, 1988.

———. *Blues, Ideology, and Afro-American Literature: A Vernacular Theory.* Chicago: U of Chicago P, 1984.

———. *A Many-Colored Coat of Dreams: The Poetry of Countee Cullen.* Detroit, MI: Broadside P, 1974.

———. *Modernism and the Harlem Renaissance.* Chicago: U of Chicago P, 1987.

———. *Workings of the Spirit: The Poetics of Afro-American Women's Writing.* Chicago: U of Chicago P, 1991.

Bassett, John E. *Harlem in Review: Critical Reactions to Black American Writers, 1917–1939.* Selinsgrove, PA: Susquehanna UP, 1992.

Berzon, Judith R. *Neither White Nor Black: The Mulatto Character in American Fiction.* New York: New York UP, 1978.

Blankenship, Russell. *American Literature as an Expression of the National Mind.* New York: H. Holt and Co., 1931.

Bone, Robert. *Down Home: A History of Afro-American Short Fiction from Its Beginnings to the End of the Harlem Renaissance.* New York: Putnam, 1975.

———. *The Negro Novel in America,* rev. ed. New Haven, CT: Yale UP, 1965.

Bontemps, Arna, ed. *The Harlem Renaissance Remembered: Essays.* New York: Dodd, 1972.

Brades, Susan Ferleger, ed. and foreword, Roger Malbert, ed. and foreword, and David A. Bailey, ed. and intro. *Rhapsodies in Black: Art of the Harlem Renaissance.* Berkeley, CA: U of California P, 1997.

Brawley, Benjamin. *The Negro Genius: A New Appraisal of the Achievement of the American Negro in Literature and Fine Arts.* New York: Dodd, 1937.

Bronz, Stephen H. *Roots of Negro Racial Consciousness: The 1920's: Three Harlem Renaissance Authors.* New York: Libra, 1964.

Brown, Sterling A. *The Negro in American Fiction.* 1937. New York: Arno, 1969 (with *Negro Poetry and Drama*).

———. *Negro Poetry and Drama.* 1937. New York: Arno, 1969 (with *The Negro in American Fiction*).

Browne, Claude. *Manchild in the Promised Land.* New York: Macmillan, 1965.

Calverton, V. F. *Anthology of American Negro Literature.* New York: The Modern Library, 1929.

Carby, Hazel. *Reconstructing Womanhood: The Emergence of the Afro-American Woman Novelist.* New York: Oxford UP, 1987.

Cooper, Wayne F. *Claude McKay: Rebel Sojourner in the Harlem Renaissance: A Biography.* 1987. New York: Schocken Books, 1990.

Cullen, Countee, ed. *Caroling Dusk: An Anthology of Verse by Negro Poets.* New York, London: Harper & Brothers, 1927.

Dallas Museum of Art. *Black Art, Ancestral Legacy: The African Impulse in African-American Art.* New York: Abrams, 1989.

Davis, Arthur P. *From the Dark Tower: Afro-American Writers 1900–1960.* Washington, D.C.: Howard UP, 1974.

DeJongh, James. *Vicious Modernism: Black Harlem and the Literary Imagination.* New York: Cambridge UP, 1990.

Douglas, Ann. *Terrible Honesty: Mongrel Manhattan in the 1920s.* New York: Farrar, Straus & Giroux, 1995.

Dowd, Jerome. *The Negro in American Life.* New York, London: Century Co., 1926.

Driskell, David C., David Levering Lewis, and Deborah Willis Ryan. *Harlem Renaissance: Art of Black America.* Intro. Mary S. Campbell. New York: Studio Museum in Harlem: Abrams, 1987.

Du Bois, W.E.B. *The Souls of Black Folk.* 1903. New York: Dodd, 1979.

duCille, Ann. *The Coupling Convention: Sex, Text, and Tradition in Black Women's Fiction.* New York: Oxford UP, 1993.

Eleazer, Robert B., ed. *Singers in the Dawn: A Brief Anthology of American Negro Poetry.* Atlanta, GA: Conference on Education and Race Relations, 1935.

Fabre, Michel. *From Harlem to Paris: Black American Writers in France, 1840–1980.* Urbana: U of Illinois P, 1991.

Fauset, Jessie Redmon. *Plum Bun.* New York: Stokes, 1929.

———. *There Is Confusion.* New York: Boni, 1924.

Fleming, Robert E. *James Weldon Johnson.* Boston: Twayne, 1987.

Floyd, Samuel A., ed. *Black Music in the Harlem Renaissance: A Collection of Essays.* New York: Greenwood P, 1990.

Ford, Nick Aaron. *The Contemporary Negro Novel: A Study in Race Relations.* 1936. College Park, MD: McGrath, 1968.

Franklin, V. P. *Living Our Stories, Telling Our Truths: Autobiography and the Making of the African-American Intellectual Tradition.* New York: Oxford UP, 1995.

French, Roy L., ed. *Recent Poetry From America, England, Ireland, and Canada.* Boston, New York: D. C. Heath and Co., 1926.

Gates, Henry Louis, Jr. *Figures in Black: Words, Signs and the "Racial" Self.* New York: Oxford UP, 1987.

———. *The Signifying Monkey: A Theory of African-American Literary Criticism.* New York: Oxford UP, 1988.

Gayle, Addison, Jr. *The Way of the New World: The Black Novel in America.* Garden City, NY: Anchor-Doubleday, 1975.

Gibson, Donald B., ed. *Modern Black Poets: A Collection of Critical Essays.* Englewood Cliffs, NJ: Prentice-Hall, 1973.

Gloster, Hugh. *Negro Voices in American Fiction.* 1948. New York: Russell, 1965.

Green, Elizabeth Lay. *The Negro in Contemporary American Literature: An Outline for Individual and Group Study.* College Park, MD: McGrath Publishing Company, 1928.

Green, J. Lee. *Time's Unfading Garden: Anne Spencer's Life and Poetry.* Baton Rouge: Louisiana State UP, 1977.

Greenberg, Cheryl. *"Or Does It Explode?": Black Harlem in the Great Depression.* New York: Oxford UP, 1991.

Hamalian, Leo, and James V. Hatch. *The Roots of African American Drama: An Anthology of Early Plays, 1858–1938.* Detroit, MI: Wayne State UP, 1991.

Harris, Trudier, ed. and fwd., and Thadious M. Davis, ed. *Afro-American Writers Before the Harlem Renaissance.* Detroit, MI: Gale, 1986.

———. *Afro-American Writers from the Harlem Renaissance to 1940.* Detroit: Gale, 1987.

Harrison, Paul Carter. *The Drama of Nommo.* New York: Grove, 1972.

Hatch, James V., and Ted Shine, eds. *Black Theatre U.S.A.: Plays by African Americans 1847 to Today.* New York: Free P, 1996.

Hatch, James V., ed. and intro., and Leo Hamalian, ed. *Lost Plays of the Harlem Renaissance: 1920–1940.* Detroit, MI: Wayne State UP, 1996.

Hatcher, Harlan. *Creating the Modern American Novel.* New York: Farrar & Rinehart, 1935.

Herskovits, Melville J. *The American Negro: A Study in Racial Crossing.* New York: A. A. Knopf, 1928.

Honey, Maureen, ed. *Shadowed Dreams: Women's Poetry of the Harlem Renaissance.* New Brunswick, NJ: Rutgers UP, 1989.

Huggins, Nathan I. *Harlem Renaissance.* New York: Oxford UP, 1971.

———, ed. *Voices from the Harlem Renaissance.* New York: Oxford UP, 1976.

Hull, Gloria. *Color, Sex, and Poetry: Three Women Writers of the Harlem Renaissance.* Bloomington: Indiana UP, 1987.

Hutchinson, George. *The Harlem Renaissance in Black and White.* Cambridge, MA: Belknap P of Harvard UP, 1995.

Ikonné, Chidi. *From Du Bois to Van Vechten: The Early New Negro Literature, 1903–1926.* Westport, CT: Greenwood P, 1981.

Inge, M. Thomas, Maurice Duke, and Jackson R. Bryer, eds. *Black American Writers: Bibliographical Essays, I: The Beginnings Through the Harlem Renaissance and Langston Hughes.* New York: St. Martin's, 1978.

Issacs, Edith J. R. *The Negro in the American Theatre.* New York: Theatre Arts, 1947.

Jackson, Blyden. *The Waiting Years: Essays on American Negro Literature.* Baton Rouge: Louisiana State UP, 1976.

Jackson, Blyden, and Louis D. Rubin, Jr. *Black Poetry in America: Two Essays in Historical Interpretation*. Baton Rouge: Louisiana State UP, 1974.

Johnson, Abby A., and Ronald M. Johnson. *Propaganda and Aesthetics: The Literary Politics of African-American Magazines in the Twentieth Century*. Amherst: U of Massachusetts P, 1991.

Johnson, James Weldon. *The Autobiography of an Ex-Coloured Man*. New York: Knopf, 1927.

———. *Black Manhattan*. New York: Alfred A. Knopf, 1940.

———. *The Book of American Negro Poetry*. New York: Harcourt, Brace and Co., 1922.

Jones, Gayl. *Liberating Voices: Oral Tradition in African American Literature*. Cambridge, MA: Harvard UP, 1991.

Kellner, Bruce. *The Harlem Renaissance: An Historical Dictionary for the Era*. 1984. New York: Methuen, 1987.

Knopf, Marcy, ed. *The Sleeper Wakes: Harlem Renaissance Stories by Women*. New Brunswick, NJ: Rutgers UP, 1993.

Kramer, Victor A., ed. *The Harlem Renaissance Re-Examined: A Revised and Expanded Edition*. Troy, NY: The Whitson Publishing Co., 1997.

Kreymborg, Alfred. *Our Singing Strength: An Outline of American Poetry 1620–1930*. New York: Coward-McCann, Inc., 1929.

Lewis, David Levering. *The Portable Harlem Renaissance Reader*. New York: Viking, 1994.

———. *When Harlem Was in Vogue*. New York, Knopf, 1981.

Littlejohn, David. *Black on White: A Critical Survey of Writing by American Negroes*. New York: Grossman, 1966.

Locke, Alain, ed. *The New Negro: An Interpretation*. New York: Albert and Charles Boni, 1925.

Martin, Tony. *African Fundamentalism: A Literary and Cultural Anthology of Garvey's Harlem Renaissance*. Dover, MA: Majority P, 1991.

———. *Literary Garveyism: Garvey, Black Arts, and the Harlem Renaissance*. Dover, MA: Majority P, 1983.

McKay, Claude. *Home to Harlem*. New York: Harper, 1928.

Miller, R. Baxter, ed. *Black American Poets Between Worlds, 1940–1960*. Knoxville: U of Tennessee P, 1986.

Mitchell, Angelyn, ed. *Within the Circle: An Anthology of African American Literary Criticism from the Harlem Renaissance to the Present*. Durham, NC: Duke UP, 1994.

Morand, Paul. *New York*. New York: H. Holt and Co., 1930.

Mullen, Edward J. *Langston Hughes in the Hispanic World and Haiti*. Hamden, Conn.: Archon Books, 1977.

Nearing, Scott. *Black America.* New York: Vanguard P, 1929.

Nelson, Cary. *Repression and Recovery: Modern American Poetry and the Politics of Cultural Memory, 1910–1945.* Madison: U of Wisconsin P, 1989.

Osofsky, Gilbert. *Harlem: The Making of a Ghetto. Negro New York, 1890–1930.* 2d. ed. Chicago: Ivan R. Dee, 1996.

Perry, Margaret. *A Bio-Bibliography of Countee P. Cullen, 1903–1946.* Westport, CT: Greenwood P, 1971.

———. *The Harlem Renaissance: An Annotated Bibliography and Commentary.* New York: Garland, 1982.

———. *Silence to the Drums: A Survey of the Literature of the Harlem Renaissance.* Westport, CT: Greenwood, 1976.

Porter, James A. *Modern Negro Art.* New York: Arno, 1969.

Rampersad, Arnold. *The Life of Langston Hughes, Vol. I: 1902–1941: I, Too, Sing America.* New York: Oxford UP, 1986.

———. *The Life of Langston Hughes, Vol. II: 1941–1967: I Dream a World.* New York: Oxford UP, 1988.

Redding, J. Saunders. *To Make a Poet Black.* 1939. College Park, MD: McGrath, 1968.

Rosenblatt, Roger. *Black Fiction.* Cambridge, MA: Harvard UP, 1974.

Roses, Lorraine Elena. *Harlem Renaissance and Beyond: Literary Biographies of 100 Black Women Writers, 1900–1945.* Boston: G. K. Hall, 1990.

Roses, Lorraine Elena, and Ruth Elizabeth Randolph, eds. *Harlem's Glory: Black Women Writing, 1900–1950.* Cambridge, MA: Harvard UP, 1996.

Rush, Theressa Gunnels, Carol Fairbanks Myers, and Esther Spring Arata. *Black American Writers Past and Present: A Biographical and Bibliographical Dictionary.* 2 vols. Metuchen, NJ: Scarecrow, 1975.

Scruggs, Charles. *The Sage in Harlem: H. L. Mencken and the Black Writers of the 1920s.* Baltimore, MD: Johns Hopkins UP, 1984.

Singh, Amritjit. *The Novels of the Harlem Renaissance: Twelve Black Writers, 1923–33.* University Park: Pennsylvania State UP, 1976.

Singh, Amritjit, William S. Shiver, and Stanley Brodwin, eds. *The Harlem Renaissance: Revaluations.* New York: Garland, 1989.

Spencer, Jon Michael. *The New Negroes and Their Music: The Success of the Harlem Renaissance.* Knoxville: U of Tennessee P, 1997.

Starke, Catherine Juanita. *Black Portraiture in American Fiction: Stock Characters, Archetypes, and Individuals.* New York: Basic, 1971.

Sudhalter, Richard M. *Lost Chords: White Musicians and Their Contribution to Jazz 1915–1943.* New York: Oxford UP, 1999.

Sundquist, Eric J. *To Wake Nations: Race in the Making of American Literature.* Cambridge, MA: Harvard UP, 1993.

Thurman, Wallace. *Infants of the Spring.* Boston: Northeastern UP, 1992.

Tracy, Steven C. *Langston Huges and the Blues.* Chicago: U of Illinois P, 1988.

Tyler, Bruce M. *From Harlem to Hollywood: The Struggle for Racial and Cultural Democracy, 1920–1943.* New York: Garland, 1992.

Van Vechten, Carl. *Nigger Heaven.* New York: Knopf, 1926.

Vincent, Theodore G. *Voices of a Black Nation: Political Journalism in the Harlem Renaissance.* San Francisco, CA: Ramparts P, 1973.

Waldron, Edward E. *Walter White and the Harlem Renaissance.* Port Washington, NY: Kennikat P, 1978.

Wall, Cheryl A. *Women of the Harlem Renaissance.* Bloomington: Indiana UP, 1995.

Washington, Mary H. *Invented Lives: Narratives of Black Women, 1860–1960.* Garden City, NY: Anchor P, 1987.

Watson, Steven. *The Harlem Renaissance: Hub of African-American Culture, 1920–1930.* New York: Pantheon Books, 1995.

Weixlmann, Joe, and Houston A. Baker, Jr., eds. *Studies in Black American Literature.* Greenwood, FL: Penkeville, 1988.

Weixlman, Joe, and Chester J. Fontenot, eds. *Belief vs. Theory in Black American Literary Criticism.* Greenwood, FL: Penkeville, 1986.

Wintz, Cary D., ed. and intro. *Analysis and Assessment, 1940–1979.* New York: Garland, 1996.

——, ed. and intro. *Analysis and Assessment, 1980–1994.* New York: Garland, 1996.

——. *Black Culture and the Harlem Renaissance.* Houston, TX: Rice UP, 1988.

——, ed. *Black Writers Interpret the Harlem Renaissance.* New York: Garland, 1996.

——, ed. *The Critics and the Harlem Renaissance.* New York: Garland, 1996.

——, ed. *The Emergence of the Harlem Renaissance.* New York: Garland, 1996.

——, ed. *The Politics and Aesthetics of "New Negro" Literature.* New York: Garland, 1996.

——, ed. *Remembering the Harlem Renaissance.* New York: Garland, 1996.

Woodson, Jon. *To Make a New Race: Gurdjieff, Toomer, and the Harlem Renaissance.* Jackson: UP of Mississippi, 1999.

Wright, John S. *A Stronger Soul Within a Finer Frame: Portraying African-Americans in the Black Renaissance.* Minneapolis: U Art Museum, U of Minnesota, 1990.

Young, James O. *Black Writers of the Thirties.* Baton Rouge: Louisiana State UP, 1973.

Dissertations

Achode, Codjo. "The Negro Renaissance from America Back to Africa: A Study of the Harlem Renaissance as a Black and African Movement." U of Pennsylvania, 1986.

Ako, Edward Oben. "The Harlem Renaissance and the Negritude Movement: Literary Relations and Influences." U of Illinois at Urbana-Champaign, 1982.

Anderson, Paul Allen. "From Spirituals to Swing: Harlem Renaissance Intellectuals, the Folk Inheritance, and the Prospects of Jazz." Cornell U, 1997.

Austin, Addell Patricia. "Pioneering Black-Authored Dramas: 1924–27." Michigan State U, 1986.

Bamikunle, Aderemi James. "The Harlem Renaissance and Negritude Poetry: The Development of Black Written Literature." U of Wisconsin–Madison, 1982.

Bernard, Emily Elaine. "Black Anxiety, White Influence: Carl Van Vechten and the Harlem Renaissance." Yale U, 1998.

Branzburg, Judith Vivian. "Women Novelists of the Harlem Renaissance: A Study in Marginality." U of Mass, 1983.

Brickhouse, Anna Campbell. "Literary Genealogy and the Politics of Revision in the American Renaissance and the Harlem Renaissance." Columbia U, 1998.

Brown, Martha Hursey. "Images of Black Women: Family Roles in Harlem Renaissance Literature." Carnegie-Mellon U, 1976.

Brown, Michael R. "Five Afro-American Poets: A History of the Major Poets and Their Poetry in the Harlem Renaissance." U of Michigan, 1971.

Carreiro, Amy Elizabeth. "African-American Writers and the Legacy of the Harlem Renaissance, 1920–1970." Oklahoma State U, 1997.

Casimir, Stephen Peter. "Folk-Life in the Harlem Renaissance Novel." McGill U (Canada), 1981.

Christian, Barbara. "Spirit Bloom in Harlem. The Search for a Black Aesthetic During the Harlem Renaissance: The Poetry of Claude McKay, Countee Cullen, and Jean Toomer." Columbia U, 1970.

Chude-Sokei, Louis Onuorah. "'The Incomprehensible Rain of Stars': Black Modernism, Black Diaspora." U of California, Los Angeles, 1995.

Cunningham, George Philbert. "Langston Hughes: A Biographical Study of the Harlem Renaissance Years, 1902–1932." Yale U, 1983.

Edwards, J. A. Craig. "Creative Reverence: Self-Defining Revisionary Discourse in the Fiction of Jessie Fauset, Nella Larsen, and Zora Neale Hurston." Indiana U, 1998.

English, Daylanne Kathryn. "Eugenics, Modernism and the Harlem Renaissance." U of Virginia, 1996.

Glenn, Rochelle Smith. "Reducing the Distance: The Rhetoric of African-American Autobiography from Slavery to the Harlem Renaissance to Civil Rights." U of Georgia, 1996.

Govan, Sandra Yvonne. "Gwendolyn Bennett: Portrait of an Artist Lost." Emory U, 1980.

Griffin, Barbara Jackson. "The Fragmented Vision of Claude McKay: A Study of His Works." U of Maryland, College Park, 1989.

Haggstrom, John Charles. "Negritude and Afro-Portuguese Poetry." U of Minnesota, 1985.

Harris, Laura Alexandra. "Troubling Boundaries: Women, Class, and Race in the Harlem Renaissance." U of California, San Diego, 1997.

Hawkins, Kimberly. "'I Heard an Angel Singing': African-American Spirituals in the Harlem Renaissance." U of California, Santa Barbara, 1997.

Helbling, Mark I. "Primitivism and the Harlem Renaissance." U of Minnesota, 1972.

Higbee, Mark David. "W. E. B. Dubois and the Problems of the Twentieth Century: Race, History, and Literature in DuBois's Political Thought, 1903–1940." Columbia U, 1995.

Hill, Anthony Duane. "J. A. Jackson's Page in 'Billboard': A Voice for Black Performance During the Harlem Renaissance Between 1920–25." New York U, 1988.

Ikonne, Chidi. "Evaluation of the Indigenousness of the Harlem Renaissance Before 'Nigger Heaven.'" U of Chicago, 1977.

Johnson, Eloise E. Warren. "A Critical Study of the Modernist Neglect of the Harlem Renaissance." Florida State U, 1993.

Jones, Sharon Lynette. "Rereading The Harlem Renaissance: The 'Folk,' 'Bourgeois,' and 'Proletarian' Aesthetics in the Fiction of Jessie Fauset, Zora Neale Hurston, and Dorothy West." U of Georgia, 1996.

Jubilee, Vincent. "Philadelphia's Afro-American Literary Circle and the Harlem Renaissance." U of Pennsylvania, 1980.

Kaplan, Carla. "Opposing Stories: Fictions of Resistance and the Case of Zora Neale Hurston." Northwestern U, 1990.

Kernodle, Tammy. "'Anything You Are Shows Up in Your Music': Mary Lou Williams and the Sanctification of Jazz." Ohio State U, 1997.

Kodat, Catherine Gunther. "Southern Modernists in Black and White: Jean Toomer, Allen Tate, William Faulkner, and Zora Neale Hurston." Boston U, 1994.

Kuenz, Jane Ellen. "Producing the New Negro: The Work of Art in the Harlem Renaissance." Duke U, 1995.

Lambert, Jasmin L. "Resisting the 'Hottentot' Body: Themes of Sexuality and Femininity in Select Plays by Female Playwrights of the Harlem Renaissance." Bowling Green State U, 1998.

Lamothe, Daphne Mary. "Ethnographic Discourse and Creole Consciousness in Harlem Renaissance Literature." U of California, Berkeley, 1997.

Lawrence, Katie Elizabeth Campbell. "Black Versus Bourgeois During the Harlem Renaissance: The Study of a Literary Conflict." U of Illinois at Urbana-Champaign, 1974.

Maxwell, William Joseph. "Dialectical Engagements: The 'New Negro' and the 'Old Left,' 1918–1940." Duke U, 1993.

McCabe, Tracy Graham. "Resisting Primitivism: Race, Gender, and Power in Modernism and the Harlem Renaissance." U of Wisconsin-Madison, 1994.

McCaskill, Barbara Ann. "To Rise Above Race: Black Women Writers and Their Readers, 1859–1939." Emory U, 1988.

McClintock, Diana Leslie. "Modernisms in the Visual Art of the Harlem Renaissance." Emory U, 1998.

McCoy, Beth Ann. "'Do I Look Like This or This?': Race, Gender, Class, and Sexuality in the Novels of Jessie Fauset, Carl Van Vechten, Nella Larsen, and F. Scott Fitzgerald." U of Delaware, 1995.

McDade, Georgia Lee. "From Hopeful to Hopeless: A Study of the Novels of Jessie Redmon Fauset." U of Washington, 1987.

McDowell, Deborah Edith. "Women on Women: The Black Woman Writer of the Harlem Renaissance." Purdue U, 1979.

McIver, Dorothy Jean Palmer. "Stepchild in Harlem: The Literary Career of Wallace Thurman." U of Alabama, 1983.

McLendon, Jacquelyn Y. "The Myth of the Mulatto Psyche: A Study of the Works of Jessie Fauset and Nella Larsen." Case Western Reserve U, 1986.

McManus, Mary Hairston. "African-American Modernism in the Novels of Jessie Fauset and Nella Larsen." U of Maryland, College Park, 1992.

Mishkin, Tracy Ann. "Black/Irish: Comparing the Harlem and Irish Renaissances." U of Michigan, 1993.

Monroe, John Gilbert. "A Record of the Black Theatre in New York City: 1920–29." U of Texas at Austin, 1980.

Musser, Judith A. "Engendering the Harlem Renaissance: The Short Stories of Marita Bonner, Zora Neale Hurston, and Other African American Women, 1921–1950." Purdue U, 1994.

Nelson, Marilyn. "Seven Library Women Whose Humane Presence Enlightened Society in the Harlem Renaissance Iconoclastic Ethos." State U of New York at Buffalo, 1996.

Newson, Adele Sheron. "An Annotated Bibliography of Critical Response to Zora Neale Hurston." Michigan State U, 1986.

Quinlan, Gloria Harrison. "A Contextual Analysis of Dorothy Rudd Moore's Song Cycle 'Sonnets on Love, Rosebuds, and Death.'" U of Texas at Austin, 1996.

Raynor, Deirdre Joyce. "Concurrent Dialogue in Novels and Plays by African-American Women from the Harlem Renaissance to the Present." U of Washington, 1997.

Reid, Margaret Ann. "A Rhetorical Analysis of Selected Black Protest Poetry of the Harlem Renaissance and of the Sixties." Indiana U of Pennsylvania, 1980.

Robinson, Anna T. "Race Consciousness and Survival Techniques Depicted in Harlem Renaissance Fiction." The Pennsylvania State U, 1973.

Russ, Robert A., III. "The Dialogics of Claude McCay." Georgia State U, 1990.

Schulz, Jennifer Lea. "Cultural Infrastructure: The Production and Circulation of the Harlem Renaissance." U of Washington, 1997.

Shuttlesworth-Davidson, Carloyn Elizabeth. "Literary Collectives of the New Negro Renaissance and the Negritude Movement." U of Michigan, 1980.

Singh, Amritjit. "The Novels of the Harlem Renaissance: A Thematic Study." New York U, 1973.

Stavney, Anne Elizabeth. "Harlem in the 1920s: A Geographical and Discursive Site of the Black and White Literary Imagination." U of Washington, 1994.

Stewart, Jeffrey Conrad. "A Biography of Alain Locke: Philosopher of the Harlem Renaissance, 1886–1930." Yale U, 1979.

Summers, Martin Anthony. "Nationalism, Race Consciousness, and the Constructions of Black Middle-Class Masculinity During the New Negro Era, 1915–1930." Rutgers, 1997.

Tillery, Tyrone. "Claude McKay: Man and Symbol of the Harlem Renaissance, 1889–1948." Kent State U, 1981.

Waldron, Edward Elvis. "Walter White and the Harlem Renaissance." Arizona State U, 1975.

West, Margaret Genevieve. "Zora Neale Hurston's Place in American Literary Culture: A Study of the Politics of Race and Gender." Florida State U, 1997.

Williams, Oscar Renal, III. "The Making of a Black Conservative: George S. Schuyler." Ohio State U, 1997.

Wintz, Cary D. "Black Writers in 'Nigger Heaven': The Harlem Renaissance." Kansas State U, 1974.

Wright, Shirley Haynes. "A Study of the Fiction of Wallace Thurman." East Texas State U, 1983.

Articles

Akam, Everett H. "Community and Cultural Crisis: The 'Transfiguring Imagination' of Alain Locke." *American Literary History* 3 (1991): 255–76.

Appiah, Kwame Anthony. "The Conservation of 'Race.'" *Black American Literature Forum* 23.1 (1989): 37–60.

Avi-Ram, Amitai F. "The Unreadable Black Body: 'Conventional' Poetic Form in the Harlem Renaissance." *Genders* 7 (1990): 32–46.

Bamikunle, Aderemi. "The Harlem Renaissance and White Critical Tradition." *CLA Journal* 29 (1985): 35–51.

Bell, Bernard. "Folk Art and the Harlem Renaissance." *Phylon* 36 (1975): 155–63.

Berg, Allison. "The New 'New Negro': Recasting the Harlem Renaissance." *College Literature* 25 (1998): 172–80.

Bontemps, Arna. "The Awakening: A Memoir." *Remembering the Harlem Renaissance.* Ed. Cary D. Wintz. New York: Garland, 1996. 235–60.

Braithwaite, William Stanley. "Alain Locke's Relationship to the Negro in American Literature." *Remembering the Harlem Renaissance.* Ed. Cary D. Wintz. New York: Garland, 1996. 420–27.

Brawley, Benjamin. "Protest and Vindication, The New Realists." *Remembering the Harlem Renaissance.* Ed. Cary D. Wintz. New York: Garland, 1996. 2–86.

Bremer, Sidney H. "Home in Harlem, New York: Lessons from the Harlem Renaissance Writers." *PMLA* 105 (1990): 47–56.

Brown, Lloyd W. "The African Heritage and the Harlem Renaissance: A Re-evaluation." *African Literature Today* 9 (1978): 1–9.

Brown, Sterling A. "Contemporary Negro Poetry (1914–1936)." *Remembering the Harlem Renaissance.* Ed. Cary D. Wintz. New York: Garland, 1996. 108–29.

——. "The New Negro in Literature (1925–1955)." *Remembering the Harlem Renaissance.* Ed. Cary D. Wintz. New York: Garland, 1996. 203–18.

——. "The Urban Scene." *Remembering the Harlem Renaissance.* Ed. Cary D. Wintz. New York: Garland, 1996. 87–106.

Byrd, Rudolph P. "Jean Toomer and the Writers of the Harlem Renaissance: Was He There with Them?" *The Harlem Renaissance: Revaluations.* Eds. Amritjit Singh, William S. Shiver, and Stanley Brodwin. New York: Garland, 1989. 209–18.

Callow, Simon. "Voodoo Macbeth." *Rhapsodies in Black: Art of the Harlem Renaissance.* Ed. and Foreword Susan Ferleger Brades and Roger Malbert, Ed. and Intro. David A. Bailey. Berkeley, CA: U of California P, 1997. 34–43.

Chapman, Abraham. "The Harlem Renaissance in Literary History." *CLA Journal* 11 (1967): 38–58.

Clarke, John H. "The Neglected Dimensions of the Harlem Renaissance." *Black World* 20 (1970): 118–29.

Coleman, Floyd, and John Adkins Richardson. "Black Continuities in the Art of the Harlem Renaissance." *Papers on Language and Literature* 12 (1976): 402–21.

Coleman, Leon. "Carl Van Vechten Presents the New Negro." *Studies in Literary Imagination* 7 (1974): 85–104.

——. "Carl Van Vechten Presents the New Negro." *The Harlem Renaissance Re-Examined.* Ed. Victor A. Kramer. New York: AMS, 1987. 107–27.

Coles, Robert A., and Diane Isaacs. "Primitivism as a Therapeutic Pursuit: Notes toward a Reassessment of Harlem Renaissance." *The Harlem Renaissance: Revaluations.* Eds. Amritjit Singh, William S. Shiver, and Stanley Brodwin. New York: Garland, 1989. 3–12.

Cooley, John. "The Emperor Jones and the Harlem Renaissance." *Studies in the Literary Imagination* 7.2 (1974): 73–83.

——. "In Search of the Primitive: Black Portraits by Eugene O'Neill and Other Village Bohemians." *The Harlem Renaissance Re-Examined.* Ed. Victor A. Kramer. New York: AMS, 1987. 51–64.

——. "White Writers and the Harlem Renaissance." *The Harlem Renaissance: Revaluations.* Eds. Amritjit Singh, William S. Shiver, and Stanley Brodwin. New York: Garland, 1989. 13–22.

Cooney, Charles F. "Walter White and the Harlem Renaissance." *Journal of Negro History* 57 (1972): 231–40.

Davis, Arthur. "Growing Up in the New Negro Renaissance, 1920–1935." *Negro American Literature Forum* 2 (1968): 53–59.

Davis, Thadious M. "Nella Larsen's Harlem Aesthetic." *The Harlem Renaissance: Revaluations.* Eds. Amritjit Singh, William S. Shiver, and Stanley Brodwin. New York: Garland, 1989. 245–56.

——. "Southern Standard-Bearers in the New Negro Renaissance." *The History of Southern Literature.* Ed. and intro. Louis D. Rubin, eds. Blyden Jackson, S. Moore Rayburn, Lewis P. Simpson, and Thomas Daniel Young. Baton Rouge: Louisiana State UP, 1985. 291–313.

Dean, Sharon, and Erlene Stetson. "Flower-Dust and Springtime: Harlem Renaissance Women." *Radical Teacher: A Newsjournal of Socialist Theory and Practice* 18 (1980): 1–8.

DePillars, Murry Norman. "Renaissance to Renaissance: Thou Shall Have No Other Gods Before Me." *Minority Voices: An Interdisciplinary Journal of Literature & the Arts* 4 (1980): 39–48.

Diawara, Manthia. "The Absent One: The Avant-Garde and the Black Imaginary in 'Looking for Langston.'" *Wide Angle: A Quarterly Journal of Film History, Theory, and Criticism* 13.3–4 (1991): 96–109.

Diepeveen, Leonard. "Folktales in the Harlem Renaissance." *American Literature* 58 (1986): 64–81.

Dunbar, Nelson. "Negro Literature for Negro Pupils." *Southern Workman* 51.2 (1922): 59–63.

Early, Gerald. "Three Notes Toward a Cultural Definition of the Harlem Renaissance." *Callaloo* 14 (1991): 136–49.

Emanuel, James A. "Renaissance Sonneteers." *Black World* 24 (1975): 32–45, 92–97.

Farnsworth, Robert M. "What Can a Poet Do? Langston Hughes and M. B. Tolson." *New Letters: A Magazine of Fine Writing* 48.1 (1981): 19–29.

Farrison, W. Edward. "Langston Hughes: Poet of the Negro Renaissance." *CLA Journal* 15 (1977): 401–10.

Fishken, Shelley Fisher. "Interrogating 'Whiteness,' Complicating 'Blackness': Remapping American Culture." *American Quarterly* 47 (1995): 428–66.

Franklin, John Hope. "The New Negro and the New Deal." *Remembering the Harlem Renaissance.* Ed. Cary D. Wintz. New York: Garland, 1996. 219–25.

Gallagher, Brian. "'About Us, For Us, Near Us': The Irish and Harlem Renaissances." *Literary Influences on African-American Writers.* Ed. Tracy Mishkin. New York: Garland, 1996. 157–70.

———. "Explorations of Black Identity from *The New Negro* to *Invisible Man.*" *Perspectives on Contemporary Literature* 8 (1983): 1–9.

Gates, Henry Louis, Jr. "Harlem on Our Minds." *Critical Inquiry* 24 (1997): 1–12.

Gayle, Addison. "The Harlem Renaissance: Towards a Black Aesthetic." *Mid-Continent American Studies Journal* 11.2 (1970): 78–87.

Gerghard, Ann. "The Emerging Self: Young-Adult and Classic Novels of the Black Experience." *English Journal* 82.5 (1993): 50–54.

Giles, Freda Scott. "Willis Richardson and Eulalie Spence: Dramatic Voices of the Harlem Renaissance." *American Drama* 5.2 (1996): 1–22.

Gilpin, Patrick. "Charles S. Johnson: Entrepreneur of the Harlem Renaissance." *Remembering the Harlem Renaissance.* Ed. Cary D. Wintz. New York: Garland, 1996. 339–70.

Goellnicht, Donald C. "Passing as Autobiography: James Weldon Johnson's *The Autobiography of an Ex-Coloured Man.*" *African American Review* 30.1 (1996): 17–35.

Gosselin, Adrienne Johnson. "Beyond the Harlem Renaissance: The Case for Black Modernist Writers." *Modern Language Studies* 26.4 (1996): 37–45.

Govan, Sandra Y. "Kindred Spirits and Sympathetic Souls: Langston Huges and Gwendolyn Bennet in the Harlem Renaissance." *Langston Hughes: The Man, His Art, and His Continuing Influence.* Ed. James C. Trotman. New York: Garland, 1995. 75–85.

Grandel, Hartmut. "The Role of Music in the Self-Reflexive Poetry of the Harlem Renaissance." *Poetics in the Poem: Critical Essays on American Self-Reflexive Poetry.* Ed. and Intro. Dorothy Z. Baker. New York: Peter Lang, 1997. 119–31.

Hart, Robert. "Black-White Literary Relations in The Harlem Renaissance." *American Literature* 44 (1973): 612–28.

Helbling, Mark. "Carl Van Vechten and the Harlem Renaissance." *Negro American Literature Forum* 10 (1976): 39–47.

Henderson, Mae Gwendoyn. "Portrait of Wallace Thurman." *Remembering the Harlem Renaissance.* Ed. Cary D. Wintz. New York: Garland, 1996. 289–312.

Henry, Katherine. "Angelina Grinke's Rhetoric of Exposure." *American Quarterly* 49.2 (1997): 328–356.

Hobson, Fred. "H. L. Mencken and the Harlem Renaissance." *Review* 7 (1985): 191–96.

Holmes, Eugene C. "Alain Locke and the New Negro Movement." *Negro American Literature Forum* 2 (1968): 60–68.

Howard, Lillie P. "'A Lack Somewhere': Nella Larsen's Quicksand and the Harlem Renaissance." *The Harlem Renaissance Re-Examined*. Ed. Victor A. Kramer. New York: AMS, 1987. 223–33.

Hudson-Weems, Clenora. "The Tripartite Plight of African-American Women as Reflected in the Novels of Hurston and Walker." *Journal of Black Studies* 20.2 (1989): 192–207.

Hughes, Langston. "Black Renaissance." *The Big Sea: An Autobiography*. 1940. New York: Hill & Wang, 1963. 221–335.

——. "Harlem Literati in the Twenties." *Remembering the Harlem Renaissance*. Ed. Cary D. Wintz. New York: Garland, 1996. 393–94.

——. "Some Practical Observations: A Colloquy." *Remembering the Harlem Renaissance*. Ed. Cary D. Wintz. New York: Garland, 1996. 131–35.

Hutchinson, George. "Nella Larsen and the Veil of Race." *American Literary History* 9 (1997): 329–49.

Jackson, Blyden. "The Harlem Renaissance." *The Comic Imagination in American Literature*. Ed. Louis D. Rubin, Jr. New Brunswick, NJ: Rutgers UP, 1973. 295–303.

——. "Renaissance in the Twenties." *The Twenties: Fiction, Poetry, Drama*. Ed. Warren French. Deland, FL: Everett, 1975. 303–316.

James, Charles L. "On the Legacy of the Harlem Renaissance: A Conversation with Arna Bontemps and Aaron Douglas." *Obsidian: Black Literature in Review* 4 (1978): 32–53.

Johnson, Abby A. "Literary Midwife: Jessie Redmon Fauset and the Harlem Renaissance." *Phylon* 39 (1978): 143–53.

Johnson, Charles S. "The Negro Renaissance and Its Significance." *Remembering the Harlem Renaissance*. Ed. Cary D. Wintz. New York: Garland, 1996. 226–34.

Jordan, June. "Where Is the Love?" *In the Memory and Spirit of Frances, Zora, and Lorraine: Essays and Interviews on Black Women and Writing*. Ed. Juliette Bowles. Washington, D.C.: Inst. for the Arts & the Humanities, Howard U, 1979.

Jubilee, Vincent. "Philadelphia's Literary Circle and the Harlem Renaissance." *The Harlem Renaissance: Revaluations*. Eds. Amritjit Singh, William S. Shiver, and Stanley Brodwin. New York: Garland, 1989. 35–47.

Kellner, Bruce. "Carl Van Vechten's Black Renaissance." *The Harlem Renaissance: Revaluations*. Eds. Amritjit Singh, William S. Shiver, and Stanley Brodwin. New York: Garland, 1989. 23–33.

———. "'Refined Racism': White Patronage in the Harlem Renaissance." *The Harlem Renaissance Re-Examined.* Ed. Victor A. Kramer. New York: AMS, 1987. 93–106.

Kent, George E. "Patterns of the Harlem Renaissance: The Fork in the Road." *Black World* (1972): 13–24, 76–80.

Knox, George. "The Harlem Renaissance Today (the 1920's 'New Negro Movement' Reviewed): Notes on a Neglected Theme." *California English Journal* 7.4 (1971): 29–33.

Krasner, David. "Whose Role Is It Anyway?: Charles Gilpin and the Harlem Renaissance." *African American Review* 29 (1995): 483–96.

Kuenz, Jane. "American Racial Discourse, 1900–1930: Schuyler's *Black No More.*" *Novel* 30.2 (1997): 170–93.

Lederer, Richard. "The Didactic and the Literary in Four Harlem Renaissance Sonnets." *English Journal* 62 (1973): 219–23.

LeSeur, Geta. "Mothers and Sons: Androgynous Relationships in Afro-West Indian and Afro-American Novels of Youth." *Western Journal of Black Studies* 16.1 (1992): 21–26.

Logan, Rayford W. "The Historical Setting of the New Negro." *Remembering the Harlem Renaissance.* Ed. Cary D. Wintz. New York: Garland, 1996. 188–95.

Lomax, Michael L. "Fantasies of Affirmation: The 1920's Novel of Negro Life." *CLA Journal* 22 (1972): 232–46.

Long, Richard A. "The Genesis of Locke's *The New Negro.*" *Black World* (Feb. 1976): 14–20.

———. "The Outer Reaches: The White Writer and Blacks in the Twenties." *The Harlem Renaissance Re-Examined.* Ed. Victor A. Kramer. New York: AMS, 1987. 43–50.

Lott, Eric. "Double V, Double-Time: Bebop's Politics of Style." *Callaloo* 11 (1988): 597–605.

Lowe, John. "Hurston, Humor, and the Harlem Renaissance." *The Harlem Renaissance Re-Examined.* Ed. Victor A. Kramer. New York: AMS, 1987. 283–313.

Lucky, Crystal J. "The Harlem Renaissance: A Revisionist Approach." *Focus on Robert Graves & His Contemporaries* 1.12 (1991): 25–29.

Marx, Edward. "Forgotten Jungle Songs: Primitivist Strategies of the Harlem Renaissance." *The Langston Hughes Review* 14 (1996): 79–93.

Maxwell, William J. "The Proletarian as New Negro: Mike Gold's Harlem Renaissance." *Radical Revisions: Rereading 1930s Culture.* Eds. Bill Mullen and Sherry Lee Linkon. Urbana: U of Illinois P, 1996. 91–119.

McCaskill, Barbara. "The Folklore of the Coasts in Black Women's Fiction of the Harlem Renaissance." *CLA Journal* 39 (1996): 273–301.

McKay, Nellie. "'What Were They Saying?': Black Women Playwrights of the Harlem Renaissance." *The Harlem Renaissance Re-Examined.* Ed. Victor A. Kramer. New York: AMS, 1987. 129–46.

McLaren, Joseph. "Early Recognitions: Duke Ellington and Langston Hughes in New York, 1920–1930." *The Harlem Renaissance: Revaluations.* Eds. Amritjit Singh, William S. Shiver, and Stanley Brodwin. New York: Garland, 1989. 195–208.

McLeod, A. L. "Claude McKay, Alain Locke, and the Harlem Renaissance." *Literary Half-Yearly* 27.2 (1986): 65–75.

Miller, Jeanne-Marie A. "Georgia Douglas Johnson and May Miller: Forgotten Playwrights of the New Negro Renaissance." *CLA Journal* 33 (1990): 349–66.

Miller, Nina. "Femininity, Publicity, and the Class Division of Cultural Labor: Jessie Redmon Fauset's *There Is Confusion.*" *African American Review* 30.2 (1996): 205–21.

Miller, Ruth, and Peter J. Katopes. "The Harlem Renaissance: Arna W. Bontemps, Countee Cullen, James Weldon Johnson, Claude McKay, and Jean Toomer." *Black American Writers: Bibliographical Essays, I: The Beginnings Through the Harlem Renaissance and Langston Hughes.* Eds. M. Thomas Inge, Maurice Duke, and Jackson R. Bryer. New York: St. Martin's, 1978. 161–86.

Morris, Lloyd. "The Negro 'Renaissance.'" *Southern Workman* 59.2 (1930): 82–86.

Moses, Wilson J. "The Lost World of the Negro, 1895–1919: Black Literary and Intellectual Life Before the 'Renaissance.'" *Black American Literature Forum* 21 (1987): 61–84.

Mott, Christopher M. "The Art of Self-Promotion: Or, Which Self to Sell? The Proliferation and Disintegration of the Harlem Renaissance." *Marketing Modernisms: Self-Promotion, Canonization, Rereading.* Ed. and Intro. Keven J. H. Dettmar and Stephen Watt. Ann Arbor: U of Michigan P, 1996.

Mudimbe-Boyi, Elisabeth. "Harlem Renaissance and Africa: An Ambiguous Adventure." *The Surreptitious Speech: Presence Africaine and the Politics of Otherness, 1947–1987.* Ed. and Pref. V. Y. Mudimbe and Leopold Sedar Senghor, Ed. and Foreword. Christaine Yande Diop. Chicago: U of Chicago P, 1992. 174–84.

Napin, Winston. "Affirming Critical Conceptualism: Harlem Renaissance Aesthetics and the Formation of Alain Locke's Social Philosophy." *Massachusetts Review* 39 (1998): 93–112.

Ogren, Kathy J. "Controversial Sounds: Jazz Performance as Theme and Language in the Harlem Renaissance." *The Harlem Renaissance: Revaluations.* Eds. Amritjit Singh, William S. Shiver, and Stanley Brodwin. New York: Garland, 1989. 159–84.

Pearson, Ralph L. "Combatting Racism with Art: Charles S. Johnson and the Harlem Renaissance." *American Studies* 18 (1977): 123–34.

Perkins, Margo V. "The Achievement and Failure of Nigger Heaven: Carl Van Vechten and the Harlem Renaissance." *CLA Journal* 42 (1998): 1–23.

Perry, Margaret. "The Harlem Renaissance: Source of Information for Research." *The Harlem Renaissance: Revaluations.* Eds. Amritjit Singh, William S. Shiver, and Stanley Brodwin. New York: Garland, 1989. 297–315.

Pfeiffer, Kathleen. "Individualism, Success, and American Identity in *The Autobiography of an Ex-Coloured Man.*" *African American Review* 30.3 (1996): 403–21.

Podesta, Guido A. "An Ethnographic Reproach to the Theory of the Avant-Garde: Modernity in Latin American and the Harlem Renaissance." *Modern Language Notes* 106.2 (1991): 395–422.

Powell, Richard J. "Re/Birth of a Nation." *Rhapsodies in Black: Art of the Harlem Renaissance.* Ed. and Foreword Susan Ferleger Brades and Roger Malbert, Ed. and Intro. David A. Bailey. Berkeley, CA: U of California P, 1997. 14–33.

Primeau, Ronald. "Frank Horne and the Second Echelon Poets of the Harlem Renaissance." *Remembering the Harlem Renaissance.* Ed. Cary D. Wintz. New York: Garland, 1996. 371–91.

Rampersad, Arnold. "Langston Hughes and Approaches to Modernism in the Harlem Renaissance." *The Harlem Renaissance: Revaluations.* Eds. Amritjit Singh, William S. Shiver, and Stanley Brodwin. New York: Garland, 1989. 49–71.

Redding, J. Saunders. "The Negro Author: His Publisher, His Public and His Purse." *Remembering the Harlem Renaissance.* Ed. Cary D. Wintz. New York: Garland, 1996. 414–18.

——. "The Negro Writer—Shadow and Substance." *Remembering the Harlem Renaissance.* Ed. Cary D. Wintz. New York: Garland, 1996. 161–63.

Russ, Robert A. "The Harlem Renaissance: A Selected Bibliography." *The Harlem Renaissance Re-examined.* Ed. Victor A. Kramer. New York: AMS, 1987. 341–349.

Sato, Hiroko. "Under the Harlem Shadow: A Study of Jessie Fauset." *Remembering the Harlem Renaissance.* Ed. Cary D. Wintz. New York: Garland, 1996. 261–87.

Schmidt, Rita T. "The Fiction of Zora Neale Hurston: An Assertion of Black Womanhood." *Ilha do Desterro: A Journal of Language & Literature.* 14.2 (1985): 53–70.

Schroeder, Patricia R. "Remembering The Disremembered: Feminist Realists of the Harlem Renaissance." *Realism and the American Dramatic Tradition.* Ed. William W. Demastes. Tuscaloosa: U of Alabama P, 1996. 91–106.

Schuyler, George S. "The Negro-Art Hokum." *Nation* 122 (June 16, 1926): 662–63.

———. "Phylon Profile, XXII: Carl Van Vechten." *Remembering the Harlem Renaissance.* Ed. Cary D. Wintz. New York: Garland, 1996. 154–60.

Scott, Freida L. "Black Drama and the Harlem Renaissance." *Theatre Journal* 37 (1985): 426–39.

———. "The Star of Ethiopia: A Contribution Toward the Development of Black Drama and Theater in the Harlem Renaissance." *The Harlem Renaissance: Revaluations.* Eds. Amritjit Singh, William S. Shiver, and Stanley Brodwin. New York: Garland, 1989. 257–69.

Scruggs, Charles W. "Alain Locke and Walter White: Their Struggle for Control of the Harlem Renaissance." *Black American Literature Forum* 14 (1980): 91–99.

———. "'All Dressed Up but No Place to Go': The Black Writer and His Audience During the Harlem Renaissance." *American Literature* 48 (1977): 543–63.

———. "Crab Antics and Jacob's Ladder: Aaron Douglas's Two Views of Nigger Heaven." *The Harlem Renaissance Re-Examined.* Ed. Victor A. Kramer. New York: AMS, 1987. 149–81.

———. "H. L. Mencken and James Weldon Johnson: Two Men Who Helped Shape a Renaissance." *Critical Essays on H. L. Mencken.* Ed. Douglas C. Stenerson. Boston: Hall, 1987. 186–203.

Singh, Amritjit. "Black-White Symbiosis: Another Look at the Literary History of the 1920s." *The Harlem Renaissance Re-Examined.* Ed. Victor A. Kramer. New York: AMS, 1987. 31–42.

Singleton, Gregory Holmes. "Birth, Rebirth, and the 'New Negro' of the 1920s." *Phylon* 43 (1982): 29–45.

Slavick, William H. "Going to School to DuBose and Heyward." *The Harlem Renaissance Re-Examined.* Ed. Victor A. Kramer. New York: AMS, 1987. 65–91.

Smith, Gary. "The Black Protest Sonnet." *American Poetry* 2 (1984): 2–12.

———. "Gwendolyn Brooks's 'A Street in Bronzeville,' the Harlem Renaissance, and the Mythologies of Black Women." *Melus* 10.3 (1983): 33–46.

Smith, Raymond. "Langston Hughes: Evolution of the Poetic Persona." *The Harlem Renaissance Re-Examined.* Ed. Victor A. Kramer. New York: AMS, 1987. 235–251.

Solbrig, Ingeborg. "Herder and the 'Harlem Renaissance' of Black Culture in America: The Case of the 'Neger-Idyllen.'" *Herder Today: Contributions from the International Herder Conference, Nov. 5–8, 1987, Stanford, California.* Ed. Kurt Mueller-Vollmer. Berlin: de Gruyter, 1990. 402–14.

Spencer, Jon Michael. "The Black Church and the Harlem Renaissance." *African American Review* 30.3 (1996): 453–60.

Stepto, Robert B. "Sterling A. Brown: Outsider in the Harlem Renaissance." *The Harlem Renaissance: Revaluations*. Eds. Amritjit Singh, William S. Shiver, and Stanley Brodwin. New York: Garland, 1989. 73–81.

Stewart, Jeffrey C. "Paul Robeson and the Problem of Modernism." *Rhapsodies in Black: Art of the Harlem Renaissance*. Ed. and Foreword Susan Ferleger Brades and Roger Malbert, Ed. and Intro. David A. Bailey. Berkeley, CA: U of California P, 1997. 90–101.

Story, Ralph D. "Patronage and the Harlem Renaissance: You Get What You Pay For." *CLA Journal* 32 (1989): 284–95.

Thomas, Lorenzo. "The Bop Aesthetic and Black Intellectual Tradition." *Library Chronicle of the University of Texas at Austin*. 24 (1994): 104–17.

———. "'Classical Jazz' and the Black Arts Movement." *African American Review* 29 (1995): 237–40.

Tischler, Barbara L. "Europa Jazz in the 1920s and the Musical Discovery of Harlem." *The Harlem Renaissance: Revaluations*. Eds. Amritjit Singh, William S. Shiver, and Stanley Brodwin. New York: Garland, 1989. 185–93.

Towns, Sandra. "Our Dark-Skinned Selves: Three Women Writers of the Harlem Renaissance." *Umoja* 1.2 (1975): 5–9.

Turner, Billy Joe. "The Harlem Renaissance and the Social Commitment Theater: Parallel Lines Which Met." *Jasat (Journal of the American Studies Association of Texas*. 17 (1986): 3–9.

Turner, Darwin T. "The Harlem Renaissance: One Facet of an Unturned Kaleidoscope." *Toward a New American Literary History: Essays in Honor of Arlin Turner*. Ed. Louis J. Budd, Edwin H. Cady, and Cal L. Anderson. Durham, NC: Duke UP, 1980. 195–210.

———. "Past and Present in Negro American Drama." *Negro*
American Literature Forum 2 (1968): 26–27.

———. "W.E.B. DuBois and the Theory of a Black Aesthetic." *The Harlem Renaissance Re-Examined*. Ed. Victor A. Kramer. New York: AMS, 1987. 9–30.

Turpin, Waters E. "Four Short Fiction Writers of the Harlem Renaissance: Their Legacy of Achievement." *CLA Journal* 11 (1967): 59–72.

Tuttleton, James W. "Countee Cullen at 'The Heights.'" *The Harlem Renaissance: Revaluations*. Eds. Amritjit Singh, William S. Shiver, and Stanley Brodwin. New York: Garland, 1989. 101–37.

Valenti, Suzanne. "The Black Diaspora: Negritude in the Poetry of West Africans and Black Americans." *Phylon* 34 (1973): 390–98.

Walden, Daniel. "W. E. B. DuBois: A Renaissance Man in the Harlem Renaissance." *Minority Voices: An Interdisciplinary Journal of Literature & the Arts.* 2 (1978): 11–20.

Waldron, Edward E. "Walter White and the Harlem Renaissance: Letters from 1924–1927." *CLA Journal* 16 (1973): 438–57.

Wall, Cheryl A. "Poets and Versifiers, Signers and Signifiers: Women of the Harlem Renaissance." *Women, the Arts, and the 1920s in Paris and New York.* Ed. and Pref. Kenneth W. Wheeler and Virginia Lee Lussier, Ed. and Intro. Catharine R. Stimpson. New Brunswick, NJ: Transaction Books, 1982. 74–98.

———. "'Whose Sweet Angel Child?': Blues Women, Langston Hughes, and Writing During the Harlem Renaissance." *Langston Hughes: The Man, His Art, and His Continuing Influence.* Ed. James C. Trotman. New York: Garland, 1995. 37–50.

Whatley-Smith, Virginia. "The Harlem Renaissance and its Blues-Jazz Traditions: Harlem and its Places of Entertainment." *Obsidian II.* 11.1/2 (1996): 21–60.

Whitlow, Roger. "The Harlem Renaissance and After: A Checklist of Black Literature of the Twenties and Thirties." *Negro American Literature Forum* 7 (1973): 143–46.

Williams, John A. "The Harlem Renaissance: Its Artists, Its Impact, Its Meaning." *Black World* 20 (1970): 17–18.

Williams, Sherley Anne. "Langston Hughes and the Negro Renaissance: 'Harlem Literati in the Twenties' (1940); 'The Twenties: Harlem and Its Negritude' (1966)." *The Langston Hughes Review* 4 (1985): 37–39.

Wintz, Cary D. "Langston Hughes: A Kansas Poet in the Harlem Renaissance." *Kansas Quarterly* 7.3 (1975): 58–71.

Woods, Gregory. "Gay Re-Readings of the Harlem Renaissance Poets." *Critical Essays: Gay and Lesbian Writers of Color.* Ed. Emmanuel S. Nelson. New York: Haworth, 1993. 127–42.

Woodson, Carter G. "Some Things Negroes Need to Do." *Southern Workman* 51.1 (1922): 82–86.

Worth, Robert F. "Nigger Heaven and the Harlem Renaissance." *African American Review* 29 (1995): 461–73.

Wright, Richard. "The Literature of the Negro in the United States." *Remembering the Harlem Renaissance.* Ed. Cary D. Wintz. New York: Garland, 1996. 428–59.

Young, Mary E. "Anita Scott Coleman: A Neglected Harlem Renaissance Writer." *CLA Journal* 40 (1997): 271–87.

Index

About the Author and Editor

MELVIN B. TOLSON (1898–1966), born in Moberly, Missouri, was an important yet often undervalued African American poet, journalist, and dramatist whose fame rests largely on four books of poetry: *Rendezvous with America* (1944), *Libretto for the Republic of Liberia* (1953), *A Gallery of Harlem Portraits* (1979), and *Harlem Gallery: Book I, The Curator* (1965). He also published a newspaper column, "Caviar and Cabbage," which appeared in the Washington *Tribune* from October 9, 1937 to June 24, 1944. He was named Poet Laureate of Liberia in 1947. In 1966 he received the National Institute and American Academy of Arts and Letters Award in Literature.

EDWARD J. MULLEN is Professor of Spanish at the University of Missouri–Columbia, where he has taught since 1971. He has been the coeditor of the *Afro-Hispanic Review* and has published numerous articles on Spanish American and African American literature. His previous books include *Afro-Cuban Literature: Critical Junctures* (Greenwood, 1998).

www.ingramcontent.com/pod-product-compliance
Lightning Source LLC
Chambersburg PA
CBHW060529310726
48982CB00002B/473

* 9 7 8 0 3 1 3 3 1 1 8 7 1 *